The Effective Anger Management Guide for Parents

Discover How to Manage and Calm Your Emotions; Turn Your Frustration Into Positive Parenting

Richard Bass

2 FREE Bonuses!

Receive a FREE <u>Planner for Kids</u> and a copy of the <u>Positive Discipline Playbook</u> by scanning below!

Interested in listening to the audio version while you read? Scan the code below and get access to The Effective Anger Management Guide for Parents' audio version for FREE!

Table of Contents

Introduction

The failures of our parents may become our burden, but it is our choice to continue carrying it onward into the next generation or put it down. –
Oriana Allen

Being a mom was the most challenging role Veronica had to play in her life. She grew up as an only child in a rough family environment, raised by a single working mother. Due to her mother's busy work schedule and avoidant attachment style, Veronica was often missing emotional connection. Her mother expected perfection from her, and many of the typical childish behaviors that kids naturally perform were seen as grounds for punishment.

The unconscious message that she received from an early age was that love was complicated, flawed, and unreliable.

Mimicking her mother's behaviors, Veronica grew up to be aloof and short-tempered, and she upheld an extremely high moral standard for herself and others. As a result, becoming pregnant with her daughter was difficult to accept. Ideally, she would have wanted to have her under different circumstances, like after getting married and living in a large house with a white picket fence. But unbeknownst to her, she was continuing the intergenerational cycle that her mother began.

You see, without acknowledging and healing the pain from her own childhood, Veronica could only repeat the behaviors she witnessed growing up, such as her mother's beliefs and attitudes toward life and parenting. As a parent, she could only raise her daughter the only way she knew how, which was to criticize her for making mistakes, yell at the slightest inconveniences, and expect mature behavior from a growing child.

The ball was now in Veronica's daughter's court. How would she address the intergenerational childhood trauma? Would she grow a thick skin, adopt maladaptive coping strategies, and view life in the same negative light as her mother and grandmother? If she did, she would only continue a pattern of parenting that would harm her children and the many generations to come.

When I come across a parent with anger issues, my immediate thoughts are: What kind of home environment were they raised in? And how much nurturing and affection did they receive from their parents? Anger problems, like any other behavioral issue, are a result of learned behavior (assuming that it is not a symptom of a mental health condition).

Even before a child can speak, they learn how to express fear, happiness, sadness, and anger by memorizing behaviors modeled by their parents and interpreting them as acceptable forms of relating and communicating. For example, when a child witnesses their parents yelling when they are angry, they assume that yelling is the acceptable way to express anger. This is how the chain of anger issues, and the host of harmful parenting approaches that come with them, are passed from one generation to another.

I'm curious to know what kind of home environment you were raised in and how much or little nurturing and affection you were given. Could you trace back your anger problems to one or both of your parents or even your grandparents? And does the way you approach parenting resemble the approach your parents used when raising you? The cycle of toxic parenting is intergenerational, but you can ensure that it ends with you!

This book is an anger management guide designed to help you recognize and address the triggers of your anger so you can enjoy the incredible privilege of being a parent. Your parent-child relationship has been placed under significant strain; however, by understanding and learning how to manage your anger, you can learn how to control your reactions, calm yourself down, and communicate your hurt feelings in a positive way.

However, rooting out your anger won't necessarily change your parenting style. Thus, beyond learning new coping strategies, you will also be introduced to a style of conscious parenting known as positive parenting. It is an approach to parenting that encourages parental leadership, open communication, and responsiveness to the needs of your child.

Growing up in a dysfunctional home environment, you may have never felt safe to express your thoughts and feelings to your parents or trusted them to look out for you. These could be challenges that your child is faced with right now. Positive parenting skills will teach you ways to rebuild trust with your child and be a positive role model in their life.

After reading this book, the hope is for you to walk away feeling less overwhelmed and more informed about how to address your anger issues. Hopefully, you will also understand the impact of your parenting style on your child's psychological well-being and be inspired to adopt positive parenting practices.

Chapter 1:

The Importance of Emotion—

for Parent and Child

Just like children, emotions heal when they are heard and validated. —Jill
Bolte Taylor

The Language of Validation

Emotional validation is the ability to recognize, understand, and
accept another person's emotional experience. This doesn't
mean that you need to be in agreement; however, validating

another's emotions shows that you understand the impact of what they are feeling. In the parent-child relationship, emotional validation is about accepting the range of emotions a child may display or express and being able to make them feel seen and heard.

A child who is emotionally validated from a young age grows up feeling comfortable expressing their feelings. They have learned that there are no "bad" or inappropriate emotions, but instead that there are healthy and unhealthy ways of expressing emotions. Feeling seen and understood helps the child connect with their parents and feel psychologically safe, which is to be confident in being their authentic self. You can see this as a gift that parents give their children because it ultimately encourages the child to develop self-compassion, openness, and greater empathy.

Growing up, you may have heard your parents say, "That wasn't good enough," or, "Don't be so stupid!" Hearing those words made you second-guess your thoughts and actions and feel ashamed of what you had done. This is known as emotional invalidation, something your parents may have done unintentionally. The invalidating words implied that you were flawed and that your experiences weren't true or didn't matter.

There is a specific kind of language that parents speak to validate their children. Unless you were raised by parents who knew this language, you may not know how to use it with your child. The language can be explained in the following three steps:

Step 1: Notice

When your child is visibly upset, you have a choice to make. You can either ignore the child or lean toward them. Leaning toward them involves stopping and noticing the emotions on their face. In words, this may sound like:

- "I saw how sad you were when Dad was leaving."

- "I heard that you had a rough day at school."

- "I can tell that you are upset with me."

Step 2: Acknowledge

After noticing your child's emotions, the next step is to acknowledge their experience as legitimate. The fact is their emotions are real, even if they are exaggerated or not suitable for the situation. For example, a child throwing a tantrum inside a supermarket is not appropriate; however, their rage at that moment is as real as it gets. If your child is old enough, you can ask them to share how they are feeling and simply mirror those feelings back to them.

For example, if your child says that they are upset because you yelled at them, you can acknowledge their feelings by responding with "What I hear is that you are upset with me because of how I spoke to you. Is this correct?" If your child is still very young, you can help them put a name to their emotions. You might say, "Is it true that you felt sad when I yelled at you?"

Step 3: Witness

The final step will be what your child remembers most vividly about the conversation. Witnessing is about leaning into your child's experience even more and empathizing with them. It isn't about telling them that they are right or wrong, blaming someone else, or finding ways to explain your actions. All that is required is to tune into what they are going through and feel it with them.

It isn't necessary to say anything while witnessing. Even sitting in silence together and maintaining open body language and softened facial expressions can be enough. Generally, the aim is to make your child feel justified in what they are feeling. For example, if your child is crying, you may want to give them a few more minutes to cry and express their frustration before comforting them or offering reassuring words.

It's important for your child to feel safe expressing strong emotions without fear of being shut down, ridiculed, misunderstood, or punished. If seeing them upset starts to make you feel emotional too, don't hold back. Similar to them, you deserve to let out your frustration.

What Emotional Invalidation Looks Like

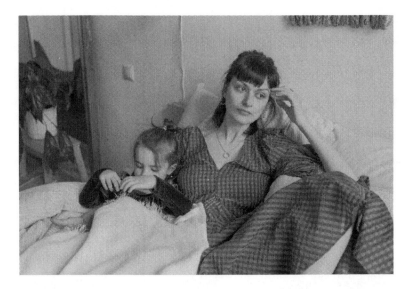

After reading about the language of validation, you may have realized that how you communicate with your child isn't the same as how most parents communicate. Maybe the norm in your household is to enter a back-and-forth argument that turns into hurling nasty insults. Or you may label your child's display of emotion as "dramatic behavior" and either retreat to your bedroom or enforce discipline.

Without being aware of it, you could be emotionally invalidating your child and making them feel guilty or ashamed for having emotional needs and desiring to express them. It could be that growing up, you were made to feel guilty or ashamed of showing emotion too, and this coping strategy stuck with you throughout your life. When you witness your child upset, it triggers a reflex inside of you to silence them or walk away.

Identifying the patterns of emotional invalidation requires you to understand the various behaviors that scream, "I don't have time for you!" Below are five common signs of emotional invalidation:

- **Your emotional experience takes priority.** If you are not in the mood to listen to what your child has to say, you will ignore them or respond in a dismissive manner. Your child often has to consider how you feel before approaching you to share any positive or negative experiences.

- **You struggle to recognize your child's boundaries.** You can sometimes undermine your child's need for space, privacy, validation, or relationships outside of the family. You believe that, as the parent, you should have unlimited access to your child and any requests for autonomy are treated with suspicion.

- **You use the silent treatment to shut down communication.** When you are feeling uncomfortable during a conversation, you have a tendency to become emotionally flat and ignore your child. This could be your way of showing disapproval for your child's actions or refusal to reach a compromise.

- **You show less affection when you are upset with your child.** Another way to convey your disapproval is by cutting back on showing your child affection. This is done to teach your child acceptable and unacceptable behaviors. The message that is conveyed is: If you don't act appropriately, then I will stop caring about you.

- **You hold your child to an unrealistically high standard.** You expect your child to think, speak, and behave in ways that you approve of. Most of the time, what you expect from them is not appropriate for their age. For example, expecting a young child to be silent while shopping is unrealistic because they are naturally buzzing with energy. When your child fails to meet this standard, you may take it as a sign of their shortcomings.

Recognizing any of these signs in yourself is the first step to increasing self-awareness and rooting out these behaviors for good. What's important is to be able to observe these behaviors without judging yourself. Judgment defeats the purpose of acknowledging and understanding where these behaviors come from, what causes you to behave that way, and what you can do to address them.

The truth is that there are no perfect parents, and many times we raise our children by borrowing beliefs and behaviors we learned growing up. The good news is that these beliefs and behaviors can be unlearned, but only if we are willing to confront ourselves.

Be Honest—How Are You Doing?

Picture this: You have three children all under the age of 10. You homeschool your seven- and five-year-olds, and the youngest is breastfeeding. Between household chores, being a teacher, and caring for an infant, there is rarely a moment during the day when you can check in with yourself and find out how you are doing.

In the evenings, your husband returns from work and entertains the kids while you prepare dinner and do a load of laundry. You can hear the youngest child screaming at the top of their lungs, not wanting to be held by Daddy. An instinctual part of you wants to run into the living room and pick them up, but you are exhausted and don't have any more "gentleness" left in you.

A thought passes through your mind: *What if I could just disappear for a few days?* You know that this isn't possible because who else would do the cleaning, cooking, nurturing, nursing, teaching, planning, chauffeuring, refereeing, and counseling at home? That's right. Nobody. The only option you have is to keep living from one moment to the next, holding onto your sanity for dear life!

Society is unforgiving when it comes to angry parents. Yell at your kid at the supermarket and watch the disgust on everyone's face. We are quick to judge the parent for having behavioral issues without understanding their backstory or how much pressure they are dealing with in their life. Yes, a parent lashing out at a child of any age is unacceptable behavior, but have we considered what the anger might be revealing about the parent's state of mind? How depressed, desperate, and discouraged they might be feeling?

Parenting is not as easy as social media makes it out to be. For the most part, it is a dirty and thankless job that starts from the moment your child is born and ends when you leave this earth. You don't receive training on how to be a parent or get an endless amount of support during the inevitable lows. It is also not possible to stop being a parent because, even when you mentally or emotionally check out, the influence you have on your child's life doesn't diminish. It is, therefore, necessary for society to show more compassion for parents, but most importantly, for parents to practice showing compassion to themselves.

Seven Signs of Parental Burnout

One of the kindest things you can do for yourself is to regularly check in on your well-being. Ask yourself, "How am I doing?" and sense what your mind and body are communicating. Daily check-ins can help you monitor your moods and respond to urgent needs, such as the need for space, sleep, food, support, or affection. The emphasis here is on responding to your needs so that you can prevent functioning on autopilot.

By doing these quick check-ins, you can also easily detect signs of parental burnout, a state of physical, mental, and emotional exhaustion related to parenting stress. Below are seven signs of parental burnout to be aware of.

1. **You often feel too tired to speak.** There are moments during the day or week when you reach a level of being overwhelmed that causes you to not feel like talking to anyone. Even when you are surrounded by family and there are opportunities to speak, you can't bring yourself to say anything.

2. **Hearing your child cry, whine, or yell makes you cringe.** You find it exhausting responding to every

strong emotion your child experiences. Sometimes, you might pretend you didn't hear them or delay responding until you summon enough strength to check on how they are doing.

3. **You depend on caffeine, cigarettes, alcohol, or prescription medication to get through the day.** If you have reached the point where you need a few cups of coffee during the day or a glass of wine every night just to feel calm, you may be dealing with a lot of stress.

4. **You have often thought about seeking medical assistance.** The idea of seeing a therapist, getting a diagnosis, or receiving any other type of medical attention has crossed your mind. This could be your mind's way of raising a red flag and signaling that something is wrong.

5. **You create excuses for not responding to your child's needs.** When your child wants to be carried, you tell them your arms are sore. When they want to play with a certain toy, you tell them it's broken. When they ask why you canceled the trip to the park, you say that the park is closed. The truth is that you don't have the energy to play and connect with your child.

6. **You find ways of getting away from your child.** There are times when you don't want to be around your child. It isn't because you don't love them, but rather that you are so frustrated by your own unmet needs. You might hide in the bedroom, take a drive to do a few errands, or spend an extra 10 minutes in the bathroom.

7. **You have unexplained fits of rage.** Even though you make an effort to keep it together, eventually the built-up frustration is unleashed. Often, the offense does not justify the huge emotional outburst, and depending on how overwhelmed you are, you might even black out for a moment. During the fit of rage, you may scream at your child, enforce harsh discipline, call them nasty names, and so on.

An overwhelmed parent is constantly exhausted. They don't have the energy to be present with their child in order to respond to their ever-changing needs and bids for love. They may also neglect their physical appearance, hygiene, and psychological well-being, which leaves them in a depressive state of mind. The anger issues and other behavioral problems that an overwhelmed parent exhibits are symptoms of physical burnout and emotional distress.

You may be completely worn out and lacking the will to show up for yourself and others. Even reading this book may take several weeks because you don't have much energy to engage in activities outside of your daily obligations. There are times when these obligations feel torturous and you doubt whether you are fit to be a parent. Please understand that what you are going through is normal and can be reversed with the right mind and body interventions.

Positive Parenting Exercise

Emotional check-ins are quick (five minutes or less) and easy to carry out wherever you may be. Follow the instructions below to administer your own check-ins:

1. **Close your eyes and tune into your body.** Notice any obvious physical sensations that may be lingering or becoming increasingly stronger. For instance, you may notice your heart beating faster, your chest tightening, your facial muscles tensing, etc. Any physical cues you pick up on should prompt you to dig deeper.

2. **Focus on slowing and lengthening your breathing.** It is difficult to check in with yourself when your mind is racing. Take slow, deep breaths through your nose for five counts, hold your breath for two counts, and gently release your breath out of your mouth for another five counts.

3. **Ask yourself, "How am I feeling right now?"** Or alternatively, you can make the question specific to any physical sensation you may have picked up on, such as, "What is my heart saying to me right now?"

4. **Think of descriptive words to describe what you are feeling.** You should be able to come up with a few emotions. If you are in a private setting, you can write these emotions down on a piece of paper. Otherwise, you can create a mental picture of what you are feeling, like a red monster to represent anger.

5. **Reflect on your day, or the past few days and weeks, and brainstorm possible triggers.** The emotion that you feel came as a result of an internal (i.e., your thoughts, emotions, and memories) or external (i.e., your relationships and environment) trigger. Identifying the trigger can be tricky, especially if there is a lot of activity happening in your life. Write

down a few possible triggers to explain what you are feeling.

After completing your check-in, you will have greater insight into your current emotional state and what might have triggered it. The power to take action and find a healthy coping strategy to return your body to a relaxed and balanced state is now in your hands!

Chapter 2:

How Were You Raised?

Once you understand what love is, you may come to the realization that your parents couldn't or didn't know how to be loving. This is one of the saddest truths you will ever have to accept. –Susan Forward

Revisiting Your Childhood Home

Take a moment to revisit your childhood home. What color was the exterior paint? What made the house stand out from all the others on the street? Recall the feeling you would get upon entering the house. Were you glad to be home, or would you instantly put your guard up?

Now picture yourself walking through the house, peeking inside each room. Which family members would you be most likely to see in the house and what would they be doing? What kinds of smells would usually fill the air as you moved from one room to the next? Could you smell musty carpet, cat litter, freshly baked bread, or Grandma's old furniture? Now try to remember if the house was quiet or noisy—if it was noisy, was it because the TV was turned to full blast, or was the noise coming from people?

Think of a typical afternoon or evening spent together as a family at home. Which family members would be present? Who would be the most relaxed and who would be the tensest? What activity would bring you all together and how did you feel while participating in the activity? How would you describe the atmosphere in the room during those moments?

Can you remember how you would walk away feeling after these family activities? What thoughts would immediately flood your mind? When you were not in the same space as your family, what would you get up to? Were you mostly alone or with other people? How would you feel being in your own space? How different was it from hanging out with your family?

Revisiting your childhood home can bring up both pleasant and upsetting memories. Some of the best and worst days of your life probably took place in the confines of that house. However, there is value in reflecting on your early memories of growing up in your family home. When you desire to trace back the origin of your beliefs, values, habits, and coping mechanisms, you can return to the house where your early childhood development happened.

The typical behaviors, expectations, traditions, and "ways of life" inside your childhood home subconsciously shaped your understanding of the world, your sense of self, and the acceptable ways of relating to other human beings. In efforts to address your anger issues and their effect on your parenting, revisiting your childhood home can reveal where, how, and why your anger came about. Answering the where, how, and why is important to getting behind your anger, finding closure, and beginning the process of healing.

Characteristics of a Dysfunctional Family

According to the American Psychological Association (APA), a dysfunctional family is defined as a family in which communication and relationships between members are impaired and therefore it is difficult to achieve closeness or allow space for members to express themselves authentically (2022).

Growing up, you may not have been aware that you were living in a dysfunctional family environment. However, what you can attest to is feeling anxious every time you returned home from school or when a certain parent would have a sudden violent outburst. The norm in your household was to expect the unexpected, making you constantly feel on edge. Below are four types of dysfunctional families that you might recognize from your early childhood experiences:

1. The Substance Abuse Family

Either one or both caregivers had a substance abuse problem, such as being addicted to drugs or alcohol. Their addiction caused a disruptive family life and the neglect of their parental responsibilities. As a child raised in this environment, you often felt physically and emotionally unsafe and full of anger and trust issues toward the neglectful (or enabling) caregiver.

2. The Conflict-Driven Family

Either one or both caregivers had an anger issue which resulted in frequent heated arguments, impulsive behaviors, harsh discipline, and long-running family feuds. Being at home felt highly stressful because you didn't know when the next dispute would erupt. To protect yourself against the caregiver's anger, you may have emotionally withdrawn, mentally dissociated, or found unhealthy ways to release your own anger (i.e., experimenting with substances, having reckless sex, running away from home, getting in fights at school, etc.).

3. The Authoritarian Family

Either one or both caregivers held high expectations that you had to meet or exceed without giving you much positive reinforcement. For example, you may have been expected to get straight As, but your parents wouldn't help you with schoolwork or attend parent-teacher conferences. The demands that were placed on you were a reflection of your caregivers' idea of a good child. When you failed to meet these demands, you would be severely punished and have your caregiver's love and attention withdrawn. Being raised in this environment led to self-esteem issues as well as trouble regulating your emotions.

4. The Emotionally Detached Family

Either one or both caregivers withdrew their warmth and affection. You may not remember receiving a hug from your parents or hearing them say, "I love you." Subconsciously, this taught you to suppress emotions and be uncomfortable or suspicious of intimacy. Not having had loving parents makes it harder for you to understand what loving parental behavior looks and feels like and makes it difficult for you to express strong emotions in a loving way. For example, when you are angry with your child, you may hurl insults and use other tactics to demean who they are as a way to express your anger. This unloving expression of anger was probably modeled by your caregivers and therefore seems normal.

By looking at these four types of dysfunctional families, we can see that there are several characteristics they have in common. These include

- **Poor communication:** Family members have a difficult time listening to each other and expressing their emotions in the appropriate manner. Some dysfunctional families may not talk to each other at all, and others may talk only when giving instructions or criticizing behavior.

- **Comparisons between family members:** Children raised in dysfunctional families are often pitted against each other. Parents may select the "golden child," who is seen as the embodiment of everything a child should be, and the rest of the children take subordinate roles.

- **Power struggles:** One or more family members compete for control in the family. This creates constant fighting and having to pick sides. Those who are being controlled may suffer from anxiety, depression, and emotional dysregulation.

- **Excessive criticism:** Children are constantly criticized for their actions or inaction. The criticism can be subtle, such as downplaying an achievement or teasing a child about their physical appearance, but it can also be direct, such as calling each other names.

- **Unpredictable behaviors:** Caregivers in dysfunctional families are often hot and cold when relating to their children. One minute, they are present and openly affectionate, and the next minute, they are absent and emotionally distant. The child may live in a constant state of anxiety or confusion, not knowing how their parents will behave next.

- **Conditional love and support:** Caregivers place conditions on love and support. For instance, a parent may only shower their child with affection when they behave in a certain way or achieve certain goals. There is usually criteria for earning the parent's love as well as behaviors that will immediately cause that love to be taken away.

The important takeaway to remember about dysfunctional families is that they reinforce dysfunctional patterns of relating to one another, which creates an unconscious toxic cycle. Members of a dysfunctional family are not always aware that how they speak to one another, resolve conflict, or show affection is unhealthy. Most of the time, they are functioning out of habit and don't understand the impact of their behaviors.

With this said, it is difficult—if not impossible—to change a dysfunctional family. However, the good news is that once you identify dysfunctional patterns, you can break them in your own life. In other words, you cannot heal your dysfunctional family, but you can break away from the cycle and relearn how to relate to others.

How the Dysfunctional Family Affected You

Being raised in a dysfunctional family affected you in ways that you may not be aware of. Many times, the effects of your upbringing are mirrored in your adult relationships or in your relationship with your child later in life. You can look at this as a good thing because once you identify toxic patterns from your childhood, you can address them immediately. Below are some of the ways that growing up in a dysfunctional family may have affected you.

1. You Tend to Feel Anxious When You Are Not in Control

Being raised in an unpredictable and chaotic home environment made you feel unsafe and neglected. You didn't trust your caregivers to be consistent in responding to your physical and emotional needs and this forced you to be self-sufficient from an early age. As an adult, you cannot stand not being informed about decisions pertaining to your life or being in control of your environment. Even something natural, like hearing your child cry, can trigger anxiety because you don't know how to control their emotional reaction.

2. You Feel Unworthy of Being a Parent

As a kid, your parents may not have provided enough emotional validation. This means that you were not reaffirmed that your feelings and perspectives matter. Subconsciously, this may have caused you to believe that you don't matter or that there is something inherently wrong with you.

Growing up, this made you doubt your own strengths and capabilities, and this is now reflected in your adult relationships—including your relationship with your child. You may look at other parents and think they are far more qualified to raise children than you, or you might think that having a troubled past makes you unfit to love and protect your child.

3. You Tend to Keep Quiet When You Should Speak

What is the one rule that children raised in dysfunctional families learn? To never speak about the family's problems to each other or outsiders. Expressing hurt feelings or raising concerns is often frowned upon because it upsets the abusive parent. Later on in life, expressing strong emotions appropriately becomes awkward and difficult.

Instead of bringing an issue up and discussing it, you might respond with the silent treatment or ignore the behavior you are witnessing. For example, if your child is painting the walls with their new set of watercolor paints, you might storm off in a rage and isolate yourself in your room instead of walking up to them and enforcing discipline.

4. You Have Difficulty Trusting Others

When you were a child, you depended on your parents to provide security, stability, and unconditional affection. However, they were unable to do so. Without developing a sense of safety in your environment and within the parent-child relationship, you grew up with trust issues. These trust issues are reflected in your adult relationships as the inability to depend on others, and you might experience strong urges to be in control in your relationships.

For example, in your relationship with your child, you might obsess over teaching them how to act because, in the back of your mind, you don't trust them to make good decisions for themselves. When they fail to meet your expectations, you might feel as though the trust you had in them has been violated, and your early childhood wounds can resurface. This might cause you to retaliate in rage, criticizing your child for making a mistake or grounding them for not doing as they were told. You may also find it difficult to move on after an argument with your child because of your inability to trust that they will do better next time.

5. You Struggle to Empathize With Others

Due to so many years of repressing painful emotions or convincing yourself that what you feel doesn't matter, you may find it difficult to empathize with other people's emotions. For example, you are able to recognize when your child is upset, but you may not know how to respond to them appropriately. When you were a child, you may have numbed or distracted yourself from feelings of sadness, and now you aren't sure how to comfort your child when they are sad. It is also possible that strong emotions make you feel uncomfortable or annoyed, and every time your child is emotional, you feel the urge to silence them by yelling, enforcing punishment, or making threats.

Four Types of Early Childhood Attachments

We have explored your childhood upbringing and looked at the type of family you came from and how the behaviors you saw growing up might have carried over into your adult relationships. However, another aspect of your upbringing that we need to consider is the type of parent-child relationship you had with your caregivers.

Why is this important? According to the attachment theory, every relationship that you form, including the relationship you have with your own child, is influenced by the first relationship you experienced as a child—the relationship that was formed with your mother.

Your mother played many different roles in your early childhood: She was your nurse, teacher, provider, and protector. Being a vulnerable infant who knew very little about the world or who you were, you relied on every cue that she gave you to feel safe and loved. The interactions between the two of you created an attachment.

Psychologists John Bowlby and Mary Ainsworth discovered four types of attachment that define the parent-child relationship. Depending on how responsive your mother was to your needs and how safe you felt expressing who you are, a specific type of attachment could have been formed. Below are the four types of attachments. Consider what they might reveal about your relationship with your mother as well as the bond you have created with your own child (Lewis, 2020):

1. Secure Attachment

If we were to select the ideal attachment style, it would be the secure attachment. It usually forms when a child is raised by a conscious and emotionally available parent. The parent is able to respond to the child's needs, create a warm and nurturing home environment, and offer plenty of positive reinforcement to support the child's self-concept.

As adults, these children grow up to have healthy self-esteem and feel confident expressing their needs in adult relationships. Since they grew up being emotionally validated, they are able to empathize with others and build mutually beneficial relationships. Secure adults are also more likely to raise secure children as a result of the lessons, beliefs, and behaviors learned in their own childhood.

2. Anxious-Insecure Attachment

When a parent is hot and cold, they have moments of being present with their child and moments where they disconnect. This behavior can cause an anxious-insecure attachment to form and make it difficult for the child to depend on their parent for their emotional needs.

One of the common causes of hot-and-cold parenting is having a demanding job, which means the parent is often away from the child for several hours, or living with a mental health condition that causes mood swings, dissociation, emotional outbursts, and manipulative tendencies, among other things.

The child grows up with trust issues, the fear of intimacy, the fear of abandonment, and not knowing how to express their emotions appropriately. For example, if the adult senses a romantic partner pulling away, they may lash out in rage or become increasingly clingy out of fear of losing them (triggered by the pain of being abandoned by their parent). As a parent, this might cause them to be overly protective or controlling of their children due to the same fear of abandonment.

3. Avoidant-Insecure Attachment

There are times when a parent has difficulty empathizing with their child's needs and their responses to them may be invalidating or insensitive, dismissing the child's feelings and causing them to feel rejected. Alternatively, the parent might turn the tables and expect the child to be sensitive toward their needs and prioritize making them feel comfortable. This type of attachment is known as avoidant-insecure attachment, and it causes the child to completely shut off their emotions, become self-reliant, and create rigid boundaries to protect their feelings from being hurt in future relationships.

In adulthood, they often form shallow relationships where intimacy is not expected. They may struggle to express their needs and instead expect others to read their mind or sense their discomfort. As parents, they may repeat the same invalidating behaviors they experienced growing up, like threatening their child, saying no to requests, expecting obedience without offering support, and minimizing their child's feelings.

4. Disorganized-Insecure Attachment

A parent who shows atypical behavior, such as ridiculing, rejecting, or frightening their child—due to their unresolved past trauma or a mental health condition (including substance abuse)—is likely to create a disorganized-insecure attachment. When the child approaches their parent, they feel afraid because they do not know what to expect.

The reason this type of attachment is called "disorganized" is that the child often has to change their coping strategies for relating to their parent. Eventually, the child might develop behavior that creates a boundary with their parent and makes them feel somewhat safe, such as being self-reliant, refusing to speak to their parent, or becoming aggressive toward their parent.

As adults, they may develop trust issues in relationships and find it difficult to open up to others. They might also have a cynical view of intimacy, such as believing that true love doesn't exist and all human beings are selfish. As a result, they are likely to be dismissive or fearful of people.

The aim of parenting is to be there for your child. However, we know that not every parent is able to do that. The result of not being responsive and affectionate toward your child is them learning unhealthy patterns of relating to people. Instead of feeling safe, open, and confident in relationships, your child becomes distrustful, withdrawn, and afraid of getting their feelings hurt. Bowlby and Ainsworth believed that once an attachment had been formed, it will remain unchanged throughout the child's life.

However, this claim is not entirely accurate. Neuroscience shows us that learned patterns of behavior can be altered or replaced. Since your brain doesn't stop processing new information and creating new neural pathways, you can unlearn old programs and adopt new ones by noticing the problem and making different decisions.

Positive Parenting Exercise

Writing a letter to your younger self can help you work through strong emotions that have been "stuck" inside your body for many decades. Back then, you didn't have a healthy way to address your concerns or reflect on the impact of how you were raised. This exercise can trigger past trauma and pain, so you may want to discuss it with your therapist before tackling it on your own. Below are a few guidelines that can help you draft the letter:

- The letter can focus on one particular time in your childhood or touch on multiple periods.

- Reflect on your childhood experiences and how they have shaped who you are today.

- Acknowledge recurring emotions that have been consistent in your life and how these emotions emerge in your adult relationships.

- Touch on some of the lessons you have learned or are beginning to learn and any advice you would like to give the younger version of you.

- Share a few character strengths and abilities that have helped you overcome difficult moments in the past. Tell yourself how proud you are!

Chapter 3:

Understand Your Anger Issues and What Triggers You

It is the most ridiculous thing in the world that we correct our children with the same wrong behavior we're telling them not to do. –Wendy Speake

What Are Anger Issues?

Understanding the root of your anger is one thing, proactively addressing your anger is another. Anger is one of the six primary emotions that every human being can display. Not only is it natural, but it can also be a healthy way to release tension from your body and feel calm. You will often sense anger through intense physical and psychological symptoms. For instance, when you tune into your body, you might feel a tightness of the chest, rapid heart rate, stomach pains, feeling hot, or unexplained sweating. When you turn inward and reflect on your emotional experience, you might feel irritable, anxious, stressed, enraged, or guilty. Even though these physical and psychological symptoms can be painful, they are also normal.

The only unnatural thing about anger is trying to hide or deny its existence. Maybe you were told as a child that "good girls" or "good boys" don't get upset or that displays of strong emotions were seen as signs of rebellion against your parents. Later in life, you may have read pseudo-psychological books that demonize anger and offer suggestions to eliminate it for good.

As a parent, you might feel guilty whenever you get angry with your child because somewhere in the back of your mind, you think that showing anger makes you a bad parent. When you think about the meaning of "unconditional love," you may assume that it doesn't include being angry with your child and that if you feel frustrated, you must be something wrong.

It saddens me to hear parents speak about the guilt they feel whenever they get angry. This is because being angry is not where the problem lies. It is justifiable to feel angry when certain life situations don't line up with your expectations. It is an acceptable human response. The real problem lies in how you choose to express your anger.

Anger issues develop when you lose control of your anger and fail to manage when and how it is expressed. In other words, it isn't your anger that is problematic, but rather how it manifests and the negative consequences that tend to follow. Aristotle once said, "Anybody can become angry—that is easy, but to be angry with the right person and to the right degree and at the right time and for the right purpose, and in the right way—that is not within everybody's power and is not easy" (Good Reads, n.d.-b).

When you have anger issues, you find it difficult to direct your anger toward the right person, display it to the right degree, reveal it at the right time, and ensure that it is expressed for the right purpose and in the right way. As a result, you tend to express your anger in three toxic ways. The first is the common and visible display of outward aggression. You might yell, curse, scream, throw objects, or physically attack someone.

The second is an invisible display of inward aggression, which means that the anger is directed at yourself. This includes putting yourself down, self-harming, self-sabotaging, or isolating yourself from others. Lastly, anger may also be unleashed passively, which involves indirect displays of outward aggression. Anger is hidden through subtle behaviors like name-calling, mocking, sarcastic remarks, gaslighting, or giving the silent treatment.

Anger issues can sometimes stem from early childhood. For instance, there are some children who are more irritable, restless, and easily angered than others. There are also some families that are more disruptive and abusive than others, which produces children who cannot confidently identify, express, and manage their emotions.

These easily angered and emotionally dysregulated children grow up with an extremely low tolerance for distress, meaning they get triggered by any minor inconvenience or frustration in their environment. As adults, they might struggle to listen, interpret, and assess the best way to handle stressful situations—their first instinctive reaction, which was picked up during childhood, is to lash out in rage.

Risk Factors for Developing Anger Issues

When you become a parent, a new identity centered around your little one emerges. Your daily thoughts are about taking care of your child and making sure you keep them alive! Your previous self—your identity before you had a child—becomes secondary, but that doesn't mean it has disappeared. You are still "you," and the ways you cope with stress haven't changed.

When you feel angry as a parent, it may have very little to do with your child or your parenting responsibilities. The triggers of your anger might actually have more to do with your personal struggles, traumas, and disappointments. Unfortunately, the anger can be directed at the wrong people— your child or family—instead of the actual source of your pain.

It is important to understand the risk factors that can cause anger issues. Doing so can bring a sense of relief in knowing exactly what made you vulnerable to uncontrolled rage. It is also a great way to empower yourself and begin making the necessary changes to your environment so that you don't constantly feel angry. Below are some risk factors that lead to anger issues.

1. Not Getting Enough Sleep

Sleep is not a luxury; it is your body's way of replenishing energy. The consequences of a lack of sleep (or a lack of quality sleep) include physical exhaustion and low moods. Imagine driving a long distance in a car with low fuel. While the car is able to move, it isn't moving at the optimal speed, and along the way, it can experience engine problems. When you don't get enough sleep, you function like a car cruising with low fuel. You are able to drag yourself through the day but not without feeling irritable, forgetful, impatient, and distracted.

Your bedtime should not be an afterthought; it should be an important part of your day. Get yourself on a sleeping schedule to train your body how to naturally feel tired and wake up at the same time. Be intentional about how you spend the few hours before bed. Generally, your work laptop and all other technological devices should be out of sight. Engage in calming activities like taking a bath, journaling, praying, or getting quality time with your partner.

2. Consuming a Poor Diet

The food you eat contributes to your emotional well-being. Researchers at Deakin University spent three months with 67 participants who consumed poor diets and also struggled with moderate to severe depression. Their poor diets consisted of sugary, salty, and processed foods. During the trial, half of the participants were placed on a Mediterranean diet, which consisted of a high intake of raw fruits and vegetables as well as lean protein.

When the three-month period was over, those who were placed on the Mediterranean diet experienced improvements in their mental health. Approximately 32% of those who modified their diet were completely cleared of their depressive symptoms versus 8% who maintained a poor diet (Lewis, 2017).

Scientists discovered the link between processed junk foods and poor brain health long ago. Foods with low nutritional value do not contain enough of the vitamins and minerals the brain needs to produce chemicals and hormones that help you make clear and rational decisions and sustain healthy moods. The types of foods that support brain health tend to have high nutritional value. These include foods like fatty fish, poultry, eggs, leafy green vegetables, and seeds and nuts.

3. Unfair or Unattainable Expectations

The expectations you set for yourself and others can create a stressful environment and put a lot of pressure on your relationships. On an individual level, expecting to be a full-time working mom while juggling household chores and taking care of your child can easily lead to burnout and resentment.

You only have 24 hours in a day and a finite amount of energy. And I get it, you want to be the best parent for your child, a reliable employee, and a devoted spouse. But expecting yourself to be all these things at once will only lead to disappointment.

Besides self-imposed expectations, there are also societal, cultural, and religious expectations that can make you aspire to unrealistic goals. For example, society's portrayal of the ideal family might be a married couple living in an affluent part of town where the man is the breadwinner and the woman is a stay-at-home mom. If you are impressed by this standard, you will strive to create your own ideal family and become increasingly frustrated with yourself when you can't fulfill the expectation.

You may be a single working mom who feels like less of a woman because you aren't able to be at home with your kids or find a suitable life partner who can take over your family's financial obligations. Social media won't make breaking this unrealistic expectation any easier because it thrives on promoting unattainable expectations. Every time you see a photo of the so-called perfect family, you can't help but feel angry at life or yourself for falling short.

The people you connect with who embody or believe in this ideal family can also unintentionally make you feel ashamed or embarrassed for not living up to their expectations. If strong boundaries haven't been established, harsh criticism and judgmental questions can take a toll on your mental health It is important to spend more time looking at your life from your perspective rather than the perspectives of your friends, family, or community. It is true that they want the best for you, but their "best" may not be realistic or desirable for your life.

4. Disorganized Lifestyle

One of the triggers of anger is a lack of feeling in control. Your environment, especially when it is disorganized, can play a huge factor in this. As a busy parent, you can try to fit as much as you can into your day, but the danger in doing this is overwhelming yourself with tasks.

Have you ever felt stressed because you had to choose between two obligations that were equally important and had to be completed at the same time? This is the result of cramming too much on your calendar or believing in the myth about multitasking. Wanting to be known as the mom or dad who does it all only creates a chaotic lifestyle that you cannot sustain in the long run.

Simplifying your schedule brings order and balance to your day. Instead of regarding everything as a priority, you choose a few important tasks to complete and do as much as you can for the rest of the day. Restoring order and balance is also about learning to say "no" to plans that require more time or effort than you can give. The beauty of saying "no" to things that don't serve you is that it enables you to say "yes" to the things that do.

For example, you might say "no" to picking up an extra shift at work because you are saying "yes" to getting home early enough to help your child with their homework. Or you might decline an invitation to a friend's party because you desire to spend the evening practicing self-care.

5. Undiagnosed Mental Health Conditions

Your mental health can also play a role in how easily or frequently you get angry. Your moods can be affected by physical conditions, such as chronic migraines, anemia, and a poorly functioning thyroid. They can also be symptoms of an underlying mental health condition. Below are a few mental disorders that tend to trigger emotional outbursts, including anger:

- depression

- substance abuse

- bipolar disorder

- anxiety disorders

- post-traumatic stress disorder (PTSD)

- intermittent explosive disorder (IED)

- obsessive-compulsive disorder (OCD)

- attention deficit hyperactivity disorder (ADHD)

Note that none of these mental disorders can be self-diagnosed. To rule out any mental health condition, you will need to visit a licensed specialist who can complete a thorough examination.

The Seven Stages of an Anger Episode

In psychology, an "episode" is a behavior that becomes progressively intense, reaches a climax, then settles down. It is common for someone with anger issues to experience anger episodes from time to time. Their episodes are often unexpected, meaning unless you are aware of what triggers your violent rage, you will not be able to predict or prevent an episode from taking place. The progression and recession of an anger episode occur in seven stages. Below is an outline of what typically happens at each stage:

1. The Trigger

Certain events, behaviors, thoughts, or emotional experiences trigger your body's natural stress response. You might feel hyperalert, nervous, afraid, or deeply uncomfortable. Your response to the trigger is proportionate to the real or imagined threat, so typically this reaction wouldn't look out of the ordinary.

2. Surge of Anger

The threat level increases steadily, and now you might start to experience shortness of breath, accelerating heart rate, and tensing of your muscles. Your feeling of anger will start out relatively tolerable. For instance, you might express irritability or warn those around you to stop doing whatever it is that is making you upset. However, the longer the anger sits in your body, the more intense it becomes. If you don't have the appropriate emotional regulation skills, the sensation can feel overwhelming.

3. Impulse to Act

At this stage, you may feel like you want to explode as a result of how angry you are. Any attempts to calm down are futile at this point because the part of your brain responsible for logic and reasoning has switched off. You are in full survival mode and ready to attack whatever you deem threatening. Those around you might look noticeably scared, waiting for you to explode at any moment.

4. Unleashing Anger

The impulse to act will eventually lead to an emotional outburst. Your body does this so that it can relieve the built-up pressure and return to a normal state. Unleashing anger is never a pleasant experience. During this stage, you may be blacked out with rage and looking for ways to harm yourself or others. You experience a total loss of control and break out of character—becoming someone you may not even recognize. Your actions can carry serious social and relational consequences.

5. Immediate Relief

Once the eye of the storm has passed and the dust has settled, you can finally breathe a sigh of relief. All of the tension that had been accumulating in your body has been released and you don't feel triggered anymore. Even if the trigger is still within your environment, it isn't provoking the same strong response from you. Due to the exhaustion from unleashing anger, you may also feel apathetic; nothing emotionally stirs you enough to react.

6. Returning to Reality

The recovery stage can take a few hours or continue for a few days. The body works hard to return to your normal pre-anger state, but on a mental level, you may be going back and forth, thinking about the incident and what you could have done differently. Returning to reality means confronting the people you hurt and restoring order in your environment.

It is normal to feel guilt and shame when thinking about or witnessing the impact of your actions. Depending on your personality and mental health, you could also fall into what is known as postcrisis depression, which could involve feeling remorseful, isolating yourself, feeling worthless, being in denial, or blaming other people. If this postcrisis depression is not addressed, it can become a gateway to self-destructive behaviors.

7. Making New Commitments

When you have returned to reality, you can look back at the incident and reflect on your behaviors. How deeply you reflect depends on your personality, level of self-awareness, and willingness to change. To repair your relationships, it is often necessary to make amends and commit to finding better ways of controlling your anger. Whether or not you actually follow through and find better coping strategies has a lot to do with your willingness to change. When you have little interest in changing your behaviors or fail to maintain new changes, you increase the risk of an anger episode recurrence.

These seven stages of an anger episode can turn into a cycle when new commitments are not honored. Bear in mind that not everyone who fails to commit to healthier coping strategies is acting out of defiance. There are many people who have learned many lessons from their anger episodes and desire to change but cannot seem to get a grip on their triggers or calm themselves down once their anger has come full force.

The therapeutic strategies that will be presented in this book are dedicated to those people who are ready and willing to break the cycle of anger episodes and make permanent lifestyle changes.

How to Identify Emotional Triggers Instantly

You are in a playful mood and are joking around with your child. Both of you are laughing and having a special moment until something they say triggers you.

Out of nowhere, you go from calm and relaxed to ice cold, and for a few seconds, the only thing you hear are those words replaying loudly in your head. Your heart starts racing and you feel a shortness of breath. It is only a matter of minutes before the peaceful afternoon becomes chaotic.

Turning to your child, you can see the look of sheer panic on their face. They think they have done something wrong but aren't sure what it is. At that moment, the last thing you feel is sympathy for them. Fight mode has been switched on, and the only thing you want to do is verbally or physically attack them.

If you reflect back on how this emotionally charged incident began, you will notice that something triggered you. If it wasn't for the trigger, your reaction wouldn't have been so disproportionately large. Your child may not have been aware that delving into a specific topic, asking a specific question, or responding to you in a specific way would push your buttons and trigger violent rage. In fact, you probably didn't even realize just how sensitive you were to that specific trigger either.

An emotional trigger can be defined as a stimulus that provokes an intense emotional reaction within you. This stimulus can be a person, words, tone of voice, behavior, situation, or an environment that is connected to a past painful experience from which you haven't fully healed. This is why emotional triggers almost always evoke strong emotions like anger or fear.

Unfortunately, there is not much you can do to prevent yourself from getting triggered. As a protective mechanism, your body physically and emotionally reacts whenever it senses a recurrence of a past negative experience. However, being aware of your emotional triggers is better than not acknowledging them at all. Awareness of your triggers helps you learn how to manage your reactions instead of repressing them. Over time, you can become better at preempting your triggers and immediately turning to the most appropriate coping strategies to calm your emotionally charged body.

Below are four questions to ask yourself when identifying emotional triggers:

1. How Do You Feel in Your Body?

An emotional trigger often begins as a subtle physical discomfort. If you take a moment to listen to your body, you will sense changes in your physiology. For instance, if you were feeling relaxed a minute ago and all of a sudden find yourself having hot or cold flashes, heart palpitations, or trouble breathing, you may be experiencing the early signs of a trigger.

If you are not one to take notice of your physical sensations, start writing notes about how your body feels at different times of the day, when you are in various social settings, or before and after talking to certain people. Memorize these physical reactions because they can alert you to a possible trigger arising.

2. What Thoughts Are Running Through Your Head?

Remember that a trigger is your body's way of signaling potential danger. A physical trigger signals that your physical safety is at risk, whereas an emotional trigger signals that your psychological safety is at risk. Therefore, the types of thoughts that are likely to flood your mind are extreme (i.e., "My child doesn't love me"), exaggerated (i.e., "No one appreciates anything I do"), or self-deprecating (i.e., "I am the worst parent ever").

Your thoughts may also reinforce a negative story you have created about yourself, your environment, or other people. For example, if you are under the assumption that your child doesn't respect you, anytime they express strong feelings, you might take it as a sign of blatant disrespect and get emotionally triggered. Instead of removing your emotions from the equation and empathizing with your child's feelings, you suspect that their feelings are a sign of how they feel about you.

It is very difficult to be aware of every story you might be telling yourself. However, if you want to track your stories, you can write them down in your journal as you become aware of them (this is likely to occur after a conflict or an anger episode). While calming yourself down and reflecting on what transpired, take a few minutes to think about the story that may have fueled your negative thoughts, beliefs, or behaviors.

3. Who or What Is the Source of the Trigger?

Once you are aware of your physical reactions and thoughts or stories that got you emotional, you can explore what caused the trigger in the first place. Was it reading an article, hearing a certain word spoken, or being in a certain environment? You can use the five senses (sight, smell, touch, hearing, taste) to identify the trigger.

Alternatively, think about what happened moments before the first signs of physical discomfort were detected. For example, moments before your heart started beating faster, where were you? Who were you with? What was being said? What noises could you hear in the background? Who or what touched you, and how did that touch make you feel?

Once again, record the sources of your triggers—including the body sensations, emotions, thoughts, and stories that came as a result of them. After some time, you will have a list of triggers and the common patterns of behavior that accompany them.

4. What Emotional Needs Were Not Being Met?

An emotional trigger can always be traced back to unresolved trauma or pain. The reason you react so strongly when triggered is that your body feels threatened. Note that the threat may not be a reflection of what is taking place right now but rather what took place many years ago. Since your body cannot tell the difference between real and imagined danger, being reminded of past trauma can sometimes trigger strong emotions as though the trauma was happening all over again.

Whenever you detect an emotional trigger, ask yourself what need or desire is not being met. In most cases, you will find that the unmet need or desire goes back to your childhood. For example, if you are angry with your child because you feel disrespected by them, what you may need is to feel valued. This need could stem from feeling neglected, bullied, or shamed as a child.

It's important to remember that having needs and desires is perfectly human. Plus, these needs and desires are not wrong to have. As a parent, you deserve to feel accepted, loved, safe, respected, and treated fairly by your child. Therefore, instead of suppressing these needs, be open about what you are missing and would like more of in your parent-child relationship. Expressing your unmet needs and desires can prevent the impulsive negative reactions that usually follow immediately after a trigger.

Identifying emotional triggers requires you to acknowledge and accept what you are feeling. It is about exploring how certain people, situations, or environments provoke strong emotions and what unmet emotional needs could be hiding behind those strong emotions. The longer you stay in this discovery phase, the easier it becomes to manage emotional triggers and delay anger episodes. Lastly, document every sensation, thought, or behavior related to your triggers so that, over time, you can learn to preempt them.

Positive Parenting Exercise

An anger diary can help you learn about the triggers, warning signs, and common behaviors you display whenever you are angry. After you have calmed down from an anger episode, take out your journal and record your experience and the outcome of your actions. Be consistent in documenting every anger-fueled conflict for the first month so that you can start to identify common triggers. Below are examples of a blank and completed anger diary entry:

Date:	
Trigger	
Warning Signs	
Anger Response	
Outcome	

Date: 11/09/2022	
Trigger	My son walked into the house with muddy shoes.
Warning Signs	Before I got angry, I noticed my chest getting tighter, my throat feeling more constricted, and my face feeling really hot. The thought running through my head was, *How can he be so careless? It's common sense to leave your dirty shoes outside!*
Anger Response	I yelled at my son and told him to sit outside until I told him to come back inside. I felt like teaching him a harsh lesson so that he won't be so careless the next time.

Date: 11/09/2022	
Outcome	After 30 minutes, I let him back inside, but he didn't talk to me or make any eye contact for a few days. He seemed scared whenever I would call his name.

Chapter 4:

Control Your Impulses

Never give a person a piece of your mind when all you really wanted to do was give them a piece of your heart. –Shannon L. Alder

What Is Emotional Impulsivity?

So far, we have looked at how an anger episode transpires and ways to identify emotional triggers. However, that is only the tip of the iceberg. Below the surface are impulses that drive you to say things you don't mean or behave in ways that compromise your relationships with your family members.

Identifying emotional triggers early enough can prevent acting impulsively; however, as you might know, triggers occur so quickly that it is sometimes difficult to predict when they will arise. It is therefore important to learn how to control your impulses in case you are triggered and don't have enough time to manage your emotions.

Emotional impulsivity can be defined as the tendency to react impulsively whenever you experience strong emotions. For example, when you are feeling angry, you might react aggressively in front of those around you as a way to express your anger. Think of a child crying when they are tired, hungry, or uncomfortable. They cry because they are overwhelmed and don't have the right words to articulate how they are feeling.

Adults who experience emotional impulsivity are not able to weigh the consequences of their actions before they react. They act first and think about the impact of their behaviors afterward. One of the reasons for impulsiveness is not having the proper emotional regulation skills to prevent emotional outbursts. Any sudden discomfort is acted upon rather than brought to question and controlled in the appropriate manner.

Phoebe is a young mom who used to speak to her two children in any way that fit her mood. Most of the time, she spoke without weighing the consequences of her words. Whenever she wanted to correct her kids' behavior, she would mock, curse, or criticize them. Phoebe acknowledged that her words were sometimes harsh, but during her heightened state of anger, these harsh words seemed like the best way to express her intense rage.

As her children grew older, she started to notice the impact of her knee-jerk reactions. Her children became fearful of making mistakes, exploring their environment, taking risks, or being playful like other children. They displayed an indifference to interests and activities that other children enjoyed and chose instead to live within the rigid boundaries that their mother had created. On the one hand, Phoebe was happy to have seemingly well-behaved children, but on the other hand, she felt guilty for instilling fear into them, which made it hard for her children to express who they are and just be kids.

Impulsivity can bring about a sense of immediate relief when you are angry, but this instant relief comes at a price. Making quick choices that make you feel good can hurt your child in ways that only become apparent later in their life. Remember, when communicating with your child—no matter how young they are—you are talking to another human being whose subconscious mind is recording the experience and learning patterns of acceptable and unacceptable behaviors

What you say now might not seem to change your child in any noticeable way, but a few years down the line, it can become their blueprint for defining who they are and how they relate to other people.

If you are not sure whether you act impulsively or not, below are a few questions that test your level of impulsivity. Please note that these questions do not replace the need for a formal evaluation from a mental health specialist.

1. Are you someone who makes decisions on the spur of the moment?

2. Do you sometimes say whatever is on the top of your mind?

3. Reflecting on past conflicts, do you often say things you don't mean?

4. Are you someone who changes their mind based on their emotional state (i.e., when you are happy, you are

more likely to say "yes," but when you are upset, you are more likely to say "no").

5. When you are angry, do your thoughts race from one assumption to another?

6. Are you quick to give up, feel anxious, or feel hopeless when things don't work in your favor?

If we were to summarize emotional impulsivity in two typical behaviors it would be the lack of thought and self-control. This normally means that decisions are made without clear intentions or purpose. Even though reacting impulsively can bring short-term relief, over time it can damage the trust in your relationships and leave you feeling ashamed.

Strategies to Manage Impulsivity

It is important to remind yourself that you are in control of your mind—not the other way around. Your thoughts are powerless until you empower them with action. For example, you can walk past a jewelry shop, spot a beautiful diamond watch, and fantasize about stealing it. But the rational part of you would question that thought, and you would end up walking away without the watch.

Or maybe you are in a library with your kid and they start acting out. Your usual approach to discipline would be to yell at them. However, since the library is a quiet public space, the rational part of you knows that it is better to calmly get your child's attention and set boundaries.

In the heat of the moment, connect with that rational part of you that knows what is acceptable and unacceptable behavior in various situations. If you aren't sure what acceptable and unacceptable behavior looks like, think of what an integrous person would do. For instance, how would someone with great integrity handle a disrespectful teenager? Would they stoop to their level and match disrespectful behavior with more disrespectful behavior ("fighting fire with fire")? Or would they set clear boundaries with appropriate consequences?

An integrous person always asks themselves, "What kind of outcome do I want to achieve?" before assessing their options and choosing the best one. Note that their decision-making is done with a clear mind free from any biases or cognitive distortions (more on that later). Therefore, when they eventually act, they are aware of their behaviors and the impact they carry.

Think about someone in your life who you believe is a person with integrity. Look at the following scenarios and write down how you believe they would act in those situations. Record your answers on a piece of paper and reevaluate them after you have read the entire book.

- Your child screams, "I hate you!" in the middle of the supermarket because they are denied their favorite piece of candy.

- You have caught your child telling a lie about their performance at school.

- When correcting your child, they have a tendency to mock what you are saying.

- Your child refuses to participate in household chores.

Impulses are relentless, and in order to control them, you will need to experiment with several strategies. The aim is not to eliminate your impulses altogether because this might cause a lot of unnecessary resistance and relapses. Instead, whenever you sense an urge to behave a certain way, revert to one of the following strategies:

- **Look at the bigger picture.** Resist the urge to react impulsively by challenging yourself to weigh the pros and cons of your behavior. What are the best- and worst-case scenarios? How might your actions impact your child five or ten years down the line? How might the relationship with your child improve or get worse?

- **Surf the urge.** Instead of trying to suppress the urge to say or do something impulsive, acknowledge the strong thoughts or emotions without acting upon them. Simply sit with the urge and breathe through its intensity until it subsides and you can regain a sense of control.

- **Know your triggers.** Memorize your trigger words and behaviors and try to preempt situations that might trigger you. For example, if one of your triggers is being yelled at, you can stop a conversation as soon as you sense tensions rising. Excuse yourself and take a moment to calm down. You can resume the conversation once both you and the other person are feeling stable.

- **Ask for support.** Reaching out for help can be a great way to talk about your experiences managing anger and receive support from other parents or a mental health specialist who can validate what you are going through and offer valuable advice. If you cannot find physical support, search for online groups and forums where parents or individuals with similar anger management issues gather to encourage and support each other.

- **Delay your reaction.** The delay tactic is effective when stalling your reaction until you have calmed down and can think rationally about your response. When you sense an urge to react, set a timer for 10–15 minutes and distract yourself with a relaxing or positive activity. Once the 10–15 minutes are up, assess how you are feeling. If you are still feeling aroused, delay your reaction again.

Bear in mind that you will need to repeat these strategies over and over again to gradually weaken your impulses. Whatever combination of strategies you decide to use, be consistent. For example, if you decide to join a support group, try your best to attend the meetings or events regularly so you can start learning and reinforcing healthier behaviors.

Signs of Intermittent Explosive Disorder

There are times when emotional impulsivity is a sign of an anger-related condition known as intermittent explosive disorder (IED). As the name suggests, the condition is characterized by intermittent emotional outbursts, which can include violent behaviors like domestic abuse, verbal abuse, road rage, or throwing objects. The major difference between traditional impulsivity and IED is that the latter often leads to full-blown anger episodes that leave you feeling tired, embarrassed, or remorseful once you return to normal.

Intermittent outbursts happen unexpectedly and last for about 30 minutes. One of the major signs of IED is having an extremely low tolerance for frustration and being triggered any time you are under stress. In between anger episodes, you are able to behave normally with acceptable behaviors. For some people, less aggressive outbursts occasionally occur between anger episodes.

The explosive behaviors displayed during an outburst vary from person to person. Generally speaking, you may carry out a few of the following behaviors:

- engaging in heated verbal arguments

- having temper tantrums

- shoving, pushing, or slapping another person

- causing damage to property

- using weapons to cause harm

- making threats or physically assaulting another person

Each outburst may be separated by a few days, weeks, or months. They can also range in severity, and extremely explosive outbursts can lead to hurting someone badly enough that they need medical assistance.

IED can be diagnosed as early as six years old; the majority of adults diagnosed with IED tend to be under the age of 40. The condition is also more likely to affect men than women. In attempting to find the cause of IED, researchers have identified a few risk factors, which include:

- **Genetics:** IED can be passed down from one generation to another. Research has shown that about 44–72% of the likelihood of developing aggressive impulsive behavior is hereditary (Cleveland Clinic, 2022).

- **Brain development:** MRI studies have revealed that the brain structure in those with IED is slightly altered. IED has been found to affect the amygdala, which is the region of the brain responsible for cognitive, emotional, and behavioral processing. Additional studies have shown that the levels of serotonin produced in the brains of those with IED are lower compared to other people.

- **Social and environmental factors:** Childhood upbringing also plays a role in predicting IED. It has been found that children who grow up in verbally and physically abusive households are more vulnerable to developing IED. Having experienced or witnessed several traumatic events can also increase the risk.

If you suspect that your impulsive behavior may be a symptom of IED, reach out to a mental health professional, like a psychologist or psychiatrist, who has experience in diagnosing the condition. When diagnosing IED, doctors use the criteria stipulated in the APA's *Diagnostic and Statistical Manual of Mental Disorders* (DSM-5). They may also ask questions about your medical, career, family, and relationship history to gather more insight into your behaviors.

Techniques to Curb Impulsivity

Managing impulsivity involves taking a closer look at your thoughts and emotions. It is about understanding how what you think or feel affects your behaviors and, subsequently, those around you. Over time, this level of self-awareness and conscious effort to control your actions can help you unlearn destructive patterns and replace them with healthier patterns of thinking.

A key term that you need to learn is "emotional regulation." This term refers to a number of coping strategies or skills that help you acknowledge and accept the full range of your emotions, skillfully plan how to engage with others to achieve the best outcomes, and adjust your behaviors accordingly. Developing emotional regulation strategies or skills is seen as one of the best ways to develop self-control and adapt to stressful events.

The following sections will explore three effective techniques to curb impulsivity: mindfulness, breath work, and cognitive restructuring. All three techniques can be practiced at home and performed whenever you sense an emotional trigger.

Mindfulness

Suppressing your emotions doesn't get rid of them. They are stored inside your body and wait on the next emotional trigger to explode. The only way to overcome strong emotions is to face them head-on and understand what they might be trying to communicate to you.

Have you ever felt something but couldn't exactly describe what you were feeling? Not being able to clearly define an emotion can heighten your stress and anxiety and make it difficult to regulate your body. The benefit of labeling your emotions and having an understanding of where they might be coming from is that you can allow the emotions to flow through your body without feeling compelled to act on them.

Mindfulness is a technique that originated in the East and is used in the Western world as a type of mind therapy. The purpose of mindfulness is to train your mind to pay attention to whatever is taking place in the present moment, including both internal and external experiences. One of the easiest ways to practice mindfulness is through meditation. With your eyes closed and body relaxed, you can tune into your five senses or take some time to listen to arising thoughts and feelings.

When you are mindful of your thoughts and feelings, you allow them to come up into your awareness; be careful not to attach yourself to them but simply observe. For example, you might notice a negative thought that provokes you to take violent action. But since you are just an observer, you can watch this thought without feeling obliged to take direction from it. All you are doing is paying attention to the thought and not feeding into the story it has created.

When used to manage impulsivity, mindfulness is more than just keeping calm. It involves being aware of triggers, changes to your physical or mental state, and any strong emotions that might provoke you to react prematurely. Below are a few mindful strategies you can practice whenever you feel angry.

1. Assume the Role of Observer

Deliberately step out of your emotional experience and look at the situation as an outsider looking in. This also implies letting go of any ideas, thoughts, or beliefs you have about the situation and adopting an unbiased and objective stance. You also need to let go of any story you have created in your mind that might cause you to become emotional. Don't buy into any story that paints you as being a victim, taken for granted, disrespected, or attacked by another person.

2. Accept Your Feelings

Anger is sometimes used as a secondary emotion to hide the primary emotion that might be too painful to express. For instance, anger can hide sadness, disappointment, shame, loneliness, or feeling neglected. Part of practicing mindfulness is learning to be comfortable with your emotions and accept them for what they are.

There are no emotions that are lesser or greater than others because each emotion provides insight into your current emotional state. Therefore, even an emotion like sadness, which we tend to hide, is worth acknowledging because it communicates how you feel about a situation and what emotional needs aren't being met. You can learn to accept your feelings by labeling and owning them as yours. A good way to communicate this is by using "I feel" statements. For example, you might say, "I feel sad that we don't communicate effectively anymore."

Note that you can also feel more than one way about a situation and expressing those opposing emotions can reduce the sense of confusion around your experience. For example, you might say, "I feel sad that we don't communicate effectively anymore but also grateful that we are at least having this conversation, which marks a new beginning." Remember that human beings are complex by nature and it is okay for your emotions to be complicated too. As long as you are able to label and own your feelings, you can experience greater clarity about your emotional state.

3. Listen Mindfully

Most of the time, we listen with the intention of providing a counterargument or finding flaws in what the other person is saying. This type of listening leads to conflict and misunderstandings. Listening mindfully is about dropping your defenses during a conversation, particularly one where you seek to resolve conflict. Instead of holding tightly to your position or argument, pay attention to what the other person is saying and how they are affected by the situation. Try to forget about your perspective and imagine that you are in their shoes and experiencing life from their perspective. How do you view the situation differently?

4. Find the Quiet Space Within

When tensions are high and you are feeling extremely uncomfortable in your environment, it is a good idea to temporarily block out everything around you and find a quiet space within. Think of this quiet space as a mental place of solitude where you can retreat to calm your mind and body. Accessing this quiet space requires you to remove yourself from the chaotic environment, find a place where you can be alone, and take long, deep breaths. Continue taking deep breaths until you notice tension leaving your body and your thoughts becoming less frantic. You can stay in this quiet space for as long as you desire.

5. Practice P.E.A.C.E.

Before responding to someone, you can manage impulsivity by practicing the acronym P.E.A.C.E., which stands for

- **Pause:** Stop yourself from reacting impulsively by intentionally pausing.

- **Exhale:** Take deep breaths and tune into your body.

- **Acknowledge/Accept:** Be aware of the impact of the situation and how it might affect you and all those involved. If you need time to reflect on how you feel, excuse yourself and go into your quiet space.

- **Choose:** Tap into your rational mind and think about the most appropriate ways to respond. Remind yourself of what an integrous person would do if they were in your situation or what you desire the outcome to be.

- **Engage:** When you have chosen the right response, engage with the other person, being mindful of what you say and—most importantly—how the message is conveyed.

Breath Work

Taking deep breaths when you are feeling emotional is just as gratifying as a glass of cold water when you are parched. Even though breathing is instinctive and something you are not always aware of, it can help you regulate emotions and stay in control during stressful moments.

Breath work is a technique that involves deliberately adjusting your breathing to change your physical, mental, and emotional state. Similar to mindfulness, it has also been adopted from Eastern traditions and is used in many therapy practices. Breath work teaches you how to take intentional breaths and focus on the present moment. With each deliberate breath, you can interrupt negative thought patterns and redirect the flow of your emotions. In other words, you can talk yourself out of acting impulsively or feeding into your anger.

Another great benefit of breath work is the ability to show self-compassion during a time when you are most vulnerable. Instead of an outward focus on how others are behaving, your attention is redirected inward, and your goal becomes listening to your body and calming yourself down. After taking a few deep breaths, you can feel more connected to yourself and confident in your abilities to manage the stressful situation.

Practicing breath work is as simple as doing breathing exercises. The important thing to remember though is to breathe in through your nose and out your mouth. In general, you should aim to take long, slow breaths but avoid breathing in too much air as this can disrupt the balance of oxygen and carbon dioxide in your bloodstream. As a safety precaution, assess your physical well-being before practicing breath work. Avoid breathing exercises if you suffer from any of these conditions:

- high blood pressure

- proneness to fainting

- frequent nausea

- tightness of chest or asthma

- flu-like symptoms

When you are ready to get started with breath work, you can try out the following breathing exercises:

1. Diaphragmatic Breathing

The best way to induce a state of relaxation is to breathe from the diaphragm. This means taking deep breaths that go beyond the chest and reach the diaphragm. You will notice that as you inhale fully, your diaphragm will expand, pushing your belly out. This is a sign that you are taking a deep breath. As soon as you exhale, the diaphragm will contract and the belly will return to its normal position.

If you are a beginner, it may be easier to lie down on a flat surface, like a bed, and put one hand on your belly and another hand on your chest. Take deep breaths and make sure that your belly is expanding and contracting but your chest remains still.

2. Holotropic Breathing

This breathing exercise was created as an alternative to mood-altering drugs. The aim is to achieve a heightened state of consciousness and improve your emotional well-being by practicing repetitive breathing patterns and movements. Due to the nature of this technique, a trained breath work practitioner must facilitate your session.

3. Pranayama

Pranayama is an Eastern breathing technique that focuses on regulating breathing. It is normally practiced during yoga or meditation to control the flow of energy in your body. One of the popular pranayama techniques is called ujjayi breathing, which seeks to calm the mind and increase mental clarity.

To practice ujjayi, sit down on a chair and take a few normal breaths. When you are ready, inhale through your nose, and when you exhale, make a long "haaaaahhhh" sound. Continue to hold the exhale for as long as you can. You can also use the exhale as an opportunity to release tension from your body. When you make the "haaaaahhhh" sound, imagine that the frustration lingering inside of you is leaving your body.

4. Breath Focus

This technique incorporates focus words or positive phrases, like mantras, to induce a state of relaxation. Your focus word can be neutral or one that provokes a certain kind of emotion. For example, if you are feeling irritable, you can focus on the phrase, "I am in control," or, "This too shall pass."

To practice breath focus, sit or lie down in a comfortable position. Start by breathing normally, then switch to deep breathing (diaphragmatic breathing). With each inhale, bring up a mental picture of the focus word. Imagine that you are inhaling the positive intention. With every exhale, imagine the built-up tension leaving your body, making space for the positive thoughts and feelings you desire. You can even say to yourself, "I am exhaling negative thoughts."

5. Equal Breathing

Equal breathing focuses on inhaling and exhaling with the same length of breath. This technique can help you control and regulate your breathing, especially when you are stressed or hyperventilating. The breath length should not be too long as this might disturb the balance of oxygen and carbon dioxide in your bloodstream.

In general, each breath should be between three to five counts in length. In between the inhale and exhale breaths, you can add a pause which should be the same length too. To start off, sit down on a chair and take a few normal breaths to relax your body. When you are ready, gently inhale for three counts through your nose, hold your breath for three counts, then slowly release the air out of your mouth for another three counts. Continue this pattern—inhaling for three counts, pausing for three counts, and exhaling for three counts—until you feel calm.

Cognitive Restructuring

We have looked at how mindfulness and breath work can help you manage impulsivity by calming your mind and body and giving you enough time to think about your actions. However, to add to this, we can look at another technique, known as cognitive restructuring, which focuses on challenging impulsive thoughts.

As the name suggests, cognitive restructuring is about reframing distorted thoughts to improve your thinking patterns. It is normal to have fear-based or anger-based thoughts from time to time, like doubting your parenting abilities or wishing that you didn't have children. However, when these fear- or anger-based thoughts become the standard conclusion you draw whenever you are upset, then they start to become destructive and lead to a range of issues, like stress, anxiety, and relationship problems.

With cognitive restructuring, you acknowledge each thought and question its validity before accepting it as the truth. For example, if the thought that your child is hiding something from you suddenly crept into your mind, you would first look at the thought from different angles, asking a range of objective questions to find out how reliable the thought is. You might ask yourself the following questions:

- What triggered this thought in the first place?

- What evidence do I have to back up my claim?

- Is this thought based on facts or my emotions?

- Is this thought black-or-white when the situation is more complicated?

- Am I basing this thought on what occurred in the past or what is happening right now?

- Is there another plausible explanation that I am overlooking?

Cognitive restructuring is also useful in preventing biased thinking. Examples of biased thinking include:

- **Emotional reasoning:** Assuming that how you feel about a situation is the truth about the situation despite factual evidence.

- **Catastrophizing:** Focusing on the worst-case scenario and, as a result, blowing a situation out of proportion.

- **Black-or-white thinking:** Thinking that something or someone is either good or bad, helpful or harmful, a friend or an enemy, and neglecting to acknowledge the complexities in between.

- **Negative bias:** Placing an emphasis on the negative aspects of a situation and overlooking the positive attributes. This also causes greater sensitivity and emotional reactions to negative behaviors than to positive behaviors.

To practice cognitive restructuring, you can follow a simple exercise. First, describe the situation that is making you feel angry or stressed. Then, identify the thought or belief you have drawn and how you feel as a result. Next, think about all of the evidence that supports your thought or belief, and then think about all of the evidence that proves it to be faulty. Once you have looked at the evidence for and against your thought or belief, come up with an alternative or balanced thought or belief that is reasonable and more likely to be true. Lastly, reflect on how this alternative thought or belief makes you feel.

Below is an example of how this exercise might work in a real-life situation:

Situation: I came home to a dirty house because my teenage kids hadn't done their chores.

Thoughts: My teenagers think that if they don't do their chores, I will do them for them.

Feelings: I feel taken for granted, exhausted from yelling, and fed up with creating punishments that don't seem to change my children's behaviors.

Evidence that supports the thought: The chores haven't been done and the house still looks the same as it did this morning.

Evidence that doesn't support the thought: My children haven't outright refused to do their chores; rather, they were at school the whole day and only arrived back home a few hours ago.

Alternative/balanced thought: My children are still doing homework and taking time for themselves after their busy day at school. I will only start to panic if the chores haven't been done by the time everyone goes to bed.

Outcome: I feel more relieved knowing that my kids aren't trying to upset me.

Cognitive restructuring is about looking beyond your perspective to see a clearer picture of the situation. In order to practice this technique correctly, you must be willing to let go of being right and instead show a willingness to learn something new about yourself and others. By taking a more balanced view of a situation, you might discover that it is not as important as you made it out to be or that your emotions might have magnified the situation. Ultimately, you will be able to see behind your impulses and decide that reacting may not be worth it after all!

Positive Parenting Exercise

Mindfulness meditation is a great technique to help you identify and accept intrusive thoughts instead of denying or fighting them. With greater acceptance of your thoughts comes greater self-regulation, meaning the choice to act upon them or not is yours. Read the following guided meditation, then isolate yourself in a quiet room for 5–10 minutes and carry out the instructions.

Sit down in a comfortable position on the floor or in a chair and gently close your eyes. Breathe normally and pay attention to the natural rhythm and pace of your breath. When you are ready, prepare yourself for the equal breathing exercise. Remember, each breath and pause must be of equal length.

Take a deep breath for three counts, hold it for three counts, and release the breath for another three counts. Continue this pattern until your body feels relaxed.

Turn your focus to your mind. Imagine that it is an infinite sky with an endless amount of space and thoughts float in and out of your awareness like clouds. Pay attention to each passing cloud (thought) and deliberately slow it down. As it moves really slowly in front of you, identify what kind of thought it is and how it makes you feel. Look at the thought objectively, as though you are detached from it.

Ask questions about the thought, like where it comes from, whether it is based on facts or emotions, and what lesson it has to teach you. Observe and take in what you learn from the thought. Allow it to continue moving until it is outside of your awareness.

Take a few deep breaths and notice if there are any other thoughts coming your way. You can choose to slow down as many thoughts as you like. There may be some thoughts you look at and decide to let pass; this is okay too. You don't have to focus deeply on every thought that crosses your mind.

When you are ready, return your focus to your body and end the meditation with a diaphragmatic breathing exercise. Remember to take deep, meaningful breaths that reach your belly. As you exhale, empty your lungs of air and take a moment to pause. Continue the exercise until you are ready to complete the meditation.

Chapter 5:

Acknowledge, Control, and Empathize With Your Emotions (A.C.E.)

You'll never cross an emotional bridge, if you keep rushing back to the other side. –T.F. Hodge

Why Sharing Your Emotions Is Difficult

Anger-related outbursts arise after weeks and months of burying emotions in your chest. They are a culmination of work-related stress, parental burnout, unfulfilling relationships, the pressure to succeed, and the challenges of "keeping up" in this fast-paced modern world. With all of these issues buzzing around in your head and stirring up your heart, you are bound to reach a point where you can't hide what you are feeling any longer.

Acknowledging your strong emotions could be something you are afraid to do. Perhaps from a young age, you were conditioned to gloss over your emotions and appear to be indifferent to stressful events taking place around you. You watched and imitated how everyone else in your household handled their emotions, which often meant pushing them down and presenting a hard exterior.

Disregarding your emotions has caused you to develop the habit of bottling up your feelings. Now, even in your adulthood, giving yourself the space to notice and accept your emotions is uncomfortable. You would rather continue to act as though you are not affected by anything until a single event triggers the release of months' worth of pent-up anger.

Think of emotions as energy created inside your body to express various emotional states. When you are happy, you are compelled to laugh or smile because these actions bring up the energy of happiness. A similar thing happens when you are angry; you are compelled to release fiery energy that expresses your frustration. As a response, you might feel the urge to yell, curse, or punch a wall to show just how angry you are. Note that these are not the best ways to react to anger, but they do allow you to get the energy out.

When your body cannot release emotional energy, pressure is created within you. Many prevalent mental health conditions, such as anxiety, depression, and anger issues, are, to some extent, caused by emotional distress. Your body was never designed to hold on to strong emotions because they weaken your physiology and put your mental well-being on the line. Rather than being taught to avoid unpleasant emotions, you were supposed to learn how to experience and work through them so they can safely leave your body.

The acronym A.C.E. stands for a technique called Acknowledge, Control, and Empathize. The aim of this technique is to teach you how to become acquainted with your emotions. When you are familiar with what you are feeling and the impact those feelings have on your mind and body, you are able to self-soothe and find appropriate coping strategies to help you relax and reflect. The following sections will discuss each step and how you can practice them at home.

Step 1: Acknowledge Your Emotion

Emotional neglect is a traumatic childhood experience that occurs when you grow up in a household that fails to recognize and provide a safe space to share your thoughts and feelings. You grow up hiding your emotions, pretending to not have any emotional needs, and only showing those few emotions that are considered acceptable in your environment, like being stoic, short-tempered, sarcastic, or cynical.

Apart from how emotional neglect affects you, it also impacts the relationship you have with your emotions. For instance, you might think that it isn't safe to show vulnerability, that your feelings don't matter, or that maybe you are too sensitive, needy, or dramatic and thus unlikable or undeserving of emotional validation. As time goes on, you might start to feel ashamed of your emotions and uncomfortable whenever other people display strong emotions in front of you. With such a strained relationship with your emotions, relating to others and holding space for them becomes difficult.

There are three areas of your life that have been negatively impacted due to growing up in an emotionally neglectful environment. These areas include:

1. Emotional Intelligence

We can define emotional intelligence as the ability to identify, understand, and manage your emotions in the most appropriate way. Having emotional intelligence helps you find healthy methods of relieving stress by being able to articulate how you feel and what your needs are; it also means you are able to effectively resolve conflict with others. Experiencing emotional neglect as a child means that you were robbed of the opportunity to practice identifying, expressing, and managing your emotions. This means that you tend to find it difficult to understand your own emotions and empathize with other people's emotional experiences.

2. Self-Compassion

Since you are not always clear about what you are feeling or why you are feeling it, you may struggle to hold space for yourself. Whenever you notice a strong emotion, your tendency might be to push the emotion down without listening to how you are feeling. Again, after an explosive anger outburst, you may be quick to judge your actions harshly before reflecting on what exactly triggered you and how you can manage your triggers better the next time.

The lack of self-compassion can also impact your willingness to seek help. It may be hard for you to ask for support, share some of your personal struggles, or listen to expert advice. This goes back to the belief that your feelings don't matter and therefore you don't deserve to be heard and validated. Ironically, you may even show more compassion for other people's struggles than your own.

3. Self-Directed Anger

Even though your childhood is just a memory now and you are not always aware of the emotional neglect you are carrying, you're still living with an inner emptiness and disconnect. Whenever you sense this emptiness and disconnect, you feel ashamed for not enjoying your relationships like others. The voice of your inner critic rings loudly in your ear, telling you how worthless, ungrateful, or troubled you are. You direct your anger inward instead of acknowledging it and ultimately setting yourself free.

Fortunately, childhood emotional neglect can be healed. The process of healing begins by getting acquainted with your feelings and acknowledging what you normally choose to suppress. Below are some strategies for how to hold space for yourself and acknowledge your emotions:

- **Become curious about your emotions.** Take a deliberate pause several times a day and pay attention to how you are feeling. You may not feel much, but even those subtle emotions lingering in the background affect your overall mood and sense of well-being.

- **Expand your emotional vocabulary.** There are six primary emotions—fear, anger, joy, surprise, disgust, and sadness. These primary emotions are the roots of hundreds of secondary emotions. Instead of labeling what you are feeling as anger, learn some of the secondary emotions grouped under anger that can more specifically describe what you are feeling.

- **Meditate on the belief that you matter.** Every morning or evening, spend 10 minutes with your eyes closed and reflect on your self-worth. Visualize your ideal self, the version of you that is healed, healthy, and happy. Practice focused breathing and concentrate on the words "I am incredible." Put your hands on your heart and feel the connection to your pulse. The life flowing inside of you is an indication that you are an exceptional human being.

- **Allow yourself the opportunity to feel.** Your strong emotions are not wrong or troublesome. They arise to display your current emotional experience. Take the time to listen to what you are feeling and how those emotions are moving in your body. Remind yourself that you are safe and in control and that your strong emotions are simply providing insight into your current emotional state.

- **Write your feelings on paper.** Sometimes, the best way to acknowledge your emotions is to write about them. Transferring what you are feeling onto paper can give you perspective and help you come to terms with your current situation. Writing can also release tension from your mind and bring about a sense of calm.

- **Embrace your vulnerability.** Opening yourself up to feeling anything at all can be uncomfortable, but so can suppressing your emotions. Embrace your vulnerability by letting go of the expectations of being strong, unfeeling, or unaffected by life. You are allowed to be upset, afraid, or overwhelmed. Realize that being sensitive to emotions is a natural human experience—and one that makes life richer and more fulfilling!

Acknowledging your emotions also involves recognizing the impact of your past emotional experiences and how you may still be affected by what transpired many years ago. The truth is that the emotions you feel running through your body aren't new. You have felt these emotions throughout your life in different contexts.

For instance, it is possible that how you display anger today is linked to an incident or several incidents that made you angry many years ago. Furthermore, the way in which you manage strong emotions today, and the impulsive behaviors that are triggered, may well have to do with the coping strategies or learned unconscious behaviors you adopted in the past.

Below are a few questions you can ask yourself concerning the impact of your past emotional experiences and how they might impact the way you process and manage emotions today.

1. What Happened?

Think about a past situation that had a significant impact on you. Write down what happened, focusing on the facts rather than your interpretation of the event. Mention who was present, where you were, how the situation began and transpired, as well as the aftermath.

2. Why Did That Situation Happen?

Look at the situation objectively and think of possible reasons why the situation happened. As an adult looking back, you may be able to have a broader perspective on the possible causes than you did as a child. You are welcome to contact those who were present during the event and ask them to share their opinions on why the situation occurred.

3. How Did You Feel Emotionally?

Take your time to identify and label the emotions you felt as a result of what happened. Remember that there is a multitude of emotions and what you felt may have been more complex than anger or sadness. Explore the plethora of secondary emotions to help you identify exactly how you felt. Due to the complex nature of human beings, it is also possible that you felt contradicting emotions, like feeling resentment and admiration for your parents. It may help to write down the definitions of each emotion so you know how to describe them in the future.

4. What Urges Did You Experience?

Consider the urges you experienced as a result of how you felt. These could include physical and emotional urges as well as those you acted upon and those you managed to control. Avoid the temptation to judge yourself as you think back on how impulsive you were or felt. Remember that you did the best you could with what you knew or had access to at the time. After reflecting on your urges, compare how you behaved then to how you currently behave when you are emotionally triggered. How similar or different are your actions?

5. What Have Been the Long-Term Effects of Your Emotions?

Lastly, refer back to your answers for the third question and consider how those emotions continued to affect your life after the situation ended. What new or different ideas, thoughts, feelings, or behaviors did you adopt? Did you relate to others or manage your relationships differently? You can also assess whether your worldview changed, and if so, how your new outlook on life affected your self-esteem.

The next time you sense a strong emotion arising within you, be mindful of the fact that what you are feeling could have been triggered by a memory of a past emotional event and have very little to do with what is happening in the present moment. Sit with your feelings without judging them or allowing them to affect how you treat those around you. Remind yourself that you can always rise above your emotions once you have identified what they are and where they might be coming from.

The next step after you have acknowledged your emotions is to control them.

Step 2: Control Your Emotion

As mentioned several times in this book, there is nothing wrong with feeling angry. However, what you do when you are angry can cause significant harm in your relationships. Once you have acknowledged your anger, it is important to control what happens next so that you can safely release the fiery energy of anger in a healthy way.

There are several different coping strategies you can use to control strong emotions. We have already discussed three of them, which are practicing mindfulness, breath work, and cognitive restructuring. In this section, we will explore healthy ways to respond to your intense emotions so you can avoid impulsive behaviors. Below are three healthy ways to react to strong emotions.

1. Recognize Defensive Behavior in Yourself

Defensiveness is the opposite of openness. It is a coping strategy used to avoid engaging in emotionally charged situations. Some emotions that can trigger defensive behaviors are stress, anxiety, and feeling personally attacked. Your reaction is to protect yourself by emotionally shutting down or becoming aggressive.

It is important to catch defensiveness as soon as possible so you can immediately turn to a healthier strategy, like reframing your thoughts or taking deep, meaningful breaths—both of which encourage openness. Here are a few signs of defensive behavior to look out for:

- Being sensitive to negative feedback.

- Making excuses to avoid taking accountability.

- Passing blame to someone else.

- Displaying negative body language (i.e., crossing your arms or avoiding eye contact).

- Smiling and nodding just to get the other person to stop talking.

Another strategy to avoid defensiveness is to take precautions against triggers that make you feel defensive. For instance, there might be specific topics that you don't want to discuss with your child or questions that you don't like being asked. Write down what your triggers are and communicate them to your child or find ways of steering the conversation to another topic when you sense where it is going.

2. Say Nothing When You Are Baited

"Baiting" is when someone, perhaps your child, says something hurtful to provoke a negative reaction from you. The aim of baiting is to get under your skin and make you frustrated enough to explode. It is hard to tell when someone is baiting you, but generally, they will say words or take actions that deliberately hurt you.

Instead of walking into their trap, step away from the conversation and focus on regulating your emotions. Excuse yourself and go somewhere quiet and isolated where you can just breathe and regain a sense of control. Refuse to continue with the conversation until you are calm. It is never a good idea to speak when you are emotional because you might retaliate by finding ways to hurt the other person too. Later on, when you are back to your normal self, you can explain to them how they hurt your feelings. You might say, "I felt really disrespected when you insulted me earlier. I know you were angry, but I didn't deserve to be spoken to like that."

3. Do the Opposite of What You Would Normally Do

When you catch yourself responding to strong emotions as you usually would, stop yourself immediately. For some people, it might help to say the words "Wait!" or "Stop!" Saying these words loudly can interrupt the negative thought pattern and lead to a moment of clarity. Once you have regained control of your mind, deliberately choose to perform the opposite action.

For example, if you were about to yell, the opposite action would be to speak calmly and respectfully. If you were going to tower over your child, the opposite action would be to step back and get down on their level. You won't always catch negative reactions in time, but always celebrate the moments when you are able to stop and consciously change your behavior.

When you are confident that you have control over your emotions, the final step is to empathize.

Step 3: Empathize With Your Emotion

We are often told to empathize with other people's feelings. But in order for that to happen, we need to first get in touch with our own feelings. Self-empathy is the ability to show openness toward your own emotional experiences. It requires you to notice, accept, and respond compassionately to your suffering.

It is common to confuse self-empathy with self-pity or self-indulgence. This is partly due to how your parents responded to your emotional needs. For example, if you were told to toughen up whenever you cried out to your parents or were mocked for feeling upset, the idea of self-empathy in adulthood might seem unnecessary. However, you experience pain just like anyone else, and your emotions—even the fieriest ones—deserve to be validated and treated with kindness and respect.

Self-empathy can be the gateway to knowing yourself better and being an expert at responding to your emotional needs. It can increase your level of self-awareness and self-discipline so that when you encounter challenging situations, you have the courage to confront them head-on. True self-empathy should not be seen as pitiful or indulgent because there is nothing wrong with accepting your feelings.

Just as stepping into another person's shoes prevents you from judging them too harshly, practicing self-empathy helps you acknowledge that you are an imperfect human who is bound to make mistakes. Being an adult or a parent doesn't give you immunity from failure or having to endure suffering. Thus, your worries, traumas, and troublesome behaviors are worthy of compassion too.

Please don't get me wrong. Self-empathy doesn't excuse bad behavior or save you from taking responsibility for your actions, including apologizing when you have hurt others. What it does is remind you that making mistakes is human and you don't have to live under a blanket of shame and self-loathing because of a poor decision. Like anyone else who has made the wrong choices in life, you deserve affection even when you mess up. The best part is that you don't have to wait on others to validate your experiences—you can validate and encourage yourself!

Developing self-empathy takes time and commitment. You must be deliberate in challenging negative thoughts about yourself, identifying acts of self-sabotage or self-harm, and being the first person to stand up for yourself. Below are a few tips for increasing self-empathy.

1. Observe Your Inner Critic

It isn't realistic to think that you can completely block out your inner critic or somehow make it disappear. Negative thoughts will always find a way to appear in your mind regardless of your emotional state. The best approach to dealing with your inner critic is to observe it rather than identify with what it tells you. Yes, this implies being open and understanding toward your most self-critical thoughts!

For example, instead of saying, "I am such a failure!" you can observe the thought and say to yourself, "My mind is saying that I am a failure." You can also preempt the reaction of your inner critic when you make mistakes. For example, after catching yourself yelling at your child, you can say, "I bet my inner critic is going to judge me harshly for this!" Another strategy is to observe your inner critic and then respond with an alternative thought. Your response to "I am such a failure!" might be "My mind is saying that I am a failure, but there is so much evidence from the past week that I am actually making progress."

2. Give Yourself Props

How many times do you stop to acknowledge the positive milestones you have reached? And by positive milestones, I am not just referring to the big goals that come once in a while. I am also including the small daily wins that you achieve each day that nobody else knows about. Write a list of positive changes in your life that you are proud of. Look at this list often, especially after a setback or self-directed rage. Take a moment to consider how much you have grown as a parent by trying new strategies that are working to improve your relationship with your child.

3. Forgive Yourself

No one is born with a manual on how to live a risk-free, pain-free, and stress-free life. We all learn what works and what doesn't along the way. Parenting is one of those responsibilities that no one is equipped for. Everything you know about being a parent has been learned on the job. It is important to come to a place where you can forgive yourself for the actions you took that hurt your child or the actions you failed to take that inconvenienced them in some way.

Realize that if you knew better and had the appropriate skills, you would have done things differently. It is unfair to hold yourself to an unobtainable standard and seek perfection. You won't always make good choices for yourself and your child, but you can always learn from your mistakes and try to make better decisions next time.

4. Avoid Comparisons

Judging yourself harshly as a parent leads to making comparisons. You might compare your parenting approach to what you see on social media or read about in magazines. The standard for parenting set by society isn't one-size-fits-all. Sure, there may be some parents who fit the mold perfectly, but that doesn't mean this approach would be appropriate for your unique family.

Nobody knows your child better than you, and there isn't a better parent to raise your child than you! When your child is hurt and needs comforting, they think about you, and when they are happy and want to share their joy with someone, you are the first person who enters their mind.

Resist the urge to undermine your role as a parent or the desire to become more like someone else. If this means unfollowing social media accounts that place unreasonable pressure on you, so be it. Let your focus be on becoming the best version of yourself so you can develop a secure attachment with your child.

5. Show Yourself Compassion by Using Affirmations

If you are looking for another way to replace negative self-talk, you can practice reciting positive affirmations. Positive affirmations are statements written in the present tense that express positive intentions about your life. Instead of affirming what you dislike about yourself, you affirm what you desire or hope to embody. Positive affirmations can help you reframe life situations and look at them from a positive perspective. You can recite the following positive affirmations before you start your day, while looking at yourself in the mirror, or when you seek to calm yourself down.

- I accept the good and bad aspects of who I am.

- I am allowed to be human.

- I accept my flaws because no one is perfect.

- I learn from my mistakes.

- I deserve kindness.

- Every day is an opportunity to make better choices.

- I embrace the positive changes happening in my life.

- I make myself proud.

- I am a work in progress.

- I release myself from others' judgment.

Positive Parenting Exercise

Think about a recent conflict you entered with your child that is still causing you a lot of stress. If you can, recall the situation in your mind and travel back to the moment when you exploded in anger.

Now, repeat the following statements to yourself:

1. This situation is painful.

2. I am in a moment of suffering.

3. I am not alone at this moment.

4. Other parents feel this way too.

5. We are all dealing with struggles in life.

6. May I show myself more kindness.

7. May I learn to accept who I am.

8. May I be patient with my healing journey.

9. May I forgive myself.

10. May I face this situation with courage.

Chapter 6:

Parenting Coping Strategies

That Don't Work

What it's like to be a parent: It's one of the hardest things you'll ever do but in exchange it teaches you the meaning of unconditional love. – Nicholas Sparks

What Not to Do When You Are Angry With Your Child

Being a parent doesn't mean you will never get angry with your child. There will be many times when you feel enraged or hurt by your child's actions. Sometimes, it may not even be your child that triggers your anger but the stress that you are experiencing in other areas of your life.

When your anger isn't controlled, it can lead to making parenting mistakes, like being too harsh and saying words you don't mean. If you don't correct these mistakes and find better ways to manage your anger, your actions can cause significant harm to your child.

Many of the bad decisions you make as a parent are unintentional. They are usually driven by impulsive behaviors, poor coping strategies, and toxic parenting patterns you learned from your own childhood. It may not even dawn on you that how you communicate and discipline your child is harmful because that's how communication and discipline were carried out when you were a child.

Nevertheless, what you say—or fail to say—really matters. It matters because your actions determine how safe your child feels in your care. The lack of empathetic communication makes your child feel threatened, and your relationship becomes one they can no longer rely on. Subsequently, they may adopt unhealthy coping strategies, like lying, shutting down, developing anger issues, suppressing their emotional needs, or other forms of "acting out."

Just as there are certain things you would never say to your spouse, mother, or coworker, there are also things that you should never say to your child. There must be boundaries put in place in your parent-child relationship to ensure that conflict never reaches a point where specific destructive words or actions are taken. Below are 10 behaviors you should avoid whenever you are angry with your child.

1. Over-Disciplining

Excessive discipline occurs when yelling turns to physical abuse or uttering psychologically damaging words. There are parents who believe that over-discipline teaches a child a lesson and prevents them from engaging in undesirable behaviors in the future. But the truth is that over-disciplining instills fear in the child and leaves them feeling unloved and unwanted. It also sends the wrong message about how conflicts between people should be resolved.

2. Under-Disciplining

No discipline is just as harmful as excessive discipline. Parents serve a specific role in a child's life: to offer guidance. When a parent treats their child more like a friend, the boundaries between the child and adult become blurred, and inappropriate behaviors become permissible. In the long run, the child may exhibit behavioral issues, like back-talking, becoming aggressive, stealing, or cheating due to the lack of self-regulation taught in their early years.

3. Withdrawing Affection

There is a parenting myth that says showing your child affection spoils them. Unconditional love has never spoiled a child, nor has it caused problematic behaviors. The effects of showing your child affection are that they feel a greater sense of security and confidence in your relationship, which directly impacts their self-esteem. When affection is withdrawn as a form of punishment, your child can experience emotional distress and react in negative ways.

4. Shaming Your Child

Believe it or not, children desire respect and appreciation too. When they are shamed, they feel inadequate, humiliated, and disappointed in themselves. Putting your child down, specifically in front of others, can damage their self-confidence. In order to feel a sense of belonging, your child wants to feel loved and accepted by you. Even when they make mistakes, your child wants to be assured that your approval of them comes with no terms and conditions.

5. Making Comparisons

Another common behavior among parents is to compare their child to older or younger siblings or their peers at school. In most cases, this is done to motivate the child to behave at home or perform better at school. However, no child finds being compared to someone else encouraging. Instead, they question their self-worth and develop insecurities. Later in life, they might become people pleasers or develop what is known as imposter syndrome, the feeling of not being good enough.

6. Constant Criticizing

Negative bias is the tendency to be more sensitive to negative information than positive information. In parenting, this might show up as constant criticism regardless of what your child does. You may also be less impressed or skeptical about the positive milestones your child reaches or find a way to downplay their performance by mentioning how they could have done better. When a child is constantly criticized, they learn to avoid positive emotions, and this can eventually develop into mental health problems, such as anxiety or depression.

7. Lack of Positive Reinforcement

The purpose of healthy conflict resolution is to unpack both sides of the story and reach a mutual agreement. To do this, it is important to not treat the other person as an enemy, but rather see yourselves as allies who are solving a problem together. One harmful thing you can do during conflict is put your child down, whether it is verbally or mentally. Discouraging them and pointing out all of their weaknesses won't assist you in solving the problem—it only chips away at your child's self-belief. Your child needs positive reinforcement as motivation to repeat good behaviors and be reminded that you still love them despite what they may have done.

8. Mocking Your Child's Feelings

Children are human beings who have the ability to feel like anybody else. Of course, the concerns your child has might be different from the concerns that keep you up at night. However, the anger, happiness, loneliness, or irritability that sometimes overtakes your body are the same emotions that can come over your child. Mocking your child's feelings minimizes their emotional experiences. It says to them that their feelings are invalid or trivial. Your child may walk away feeling rejected and learn to hide their emotions out of fear of being ridiculed or turned away.

9. Violating Boundaries

Crossing your child's boundaries is a major sign of disrespect. Once again, your child is an individual whose needs may not look identical to yours. The older they get, the more preferences they will have regarding their personal space, privacy, and how they would like to spend their free time. Respecting your child's boundaries, even when you are upset, shows how much you trust and respect them. In turn, they are more likely to respect others' boundaries too.

10. Threatening Your Child

When you threaten your child, it may seem like you are giving them an option, but in reality, you are not. What you are doing is guilt-tripping them into doing what makes you happy. Your child will follow your wishes because, as the parent, you have the upper hand. However, unconsciously, you are teaching them to prioritize other people's needs and desires above their own. Later in life, they might find themselves in manipulative relationships because of their fear of saying no or standing up for themselves.

You might look at these 10 behaviors and think they aren't the worst things that could happen to your child. But imagine if your child acquired one of these behaviors and treated you and other friends and family in that manner. How would that make you feel?

Whether you are aware of it or not, your child is constantly processing and learning your behaviors. Eventually, they will start to imitate you, not because they think you are godlike, but because they genuinely believe that how you act is the appropriate way to behave.

Take a few moments and reflect on this question: Would you be proud to witness your child talk to people or resolve conflict the way you do?

Why Traditional Punishment Doesn't Work

A common misconception in parenting is that if you don't punish your children, they will grow up to become troublemakers. Traditionally, it was encouraged for children to be raised with the rod, which meant being disciplined with physical punishment. Many times, children were not even taught the significance of the rules they followed, and god forbid they questioned them.

Ted and his twin brother were part of the generations of children brought up under traditional punishment. Their father would use violent forms of punishment to correct their troublesome behaviors, but the boys didn't necessarily grow up wiser and more confident because of this. In fact, the main message ingrained in their minds was that going against the rules caused severe pain.

As an adult, Ted's twin brother completely rejected rules as a claim to freedom and found himself in trouble with the law on several occasions. Ted, on the other hand, was too afraid to go against the rules. He got a job, found a wife, and started a family—everything that society and his father would approve of. But even though he had it all, he wasn't happy. Every day, Ted was haunted by the idea of discovering who he truly was and how he desired to live.

Punishment doesn't teach a child what is right and what is wrong; it only reinforces the fear of doing what is wrong. Instilling fear in your child won't help them take responsibility for their actions and learn to regulate their emotions and behaviors. All it will do is make them walk on eggshells, afraid of the next time they make a mistake and the punishment they might face.

Author and clinical psychologist Laura Markham provides seven reasons why punishment is not a good approach to discipline (2014):

- Punishment causes a child to see their parents as the authority figure responsible for making them behave properly. They are unable to learn and take accountability for their actions because the authority figure is always there to correct them.

- Punishment places too much emphasis on the consequence of bad behavior rather than the impact of bad behavior. A child learns to fear the consequences instead of understanding why their actions are harmful.

- After receiving punishment, a child walks away feeling like they are a bad person. Having such a low view of themselves causes them to repeat the same mistakes and feel worse about themselves. The cycle of feeling guilty, repeating mistakes, and experiencing more guilt continues.

- Since punishment causes physical and emotional pain, a child learns to avoid it by being dishonest. They might hide their mistakes, blame somebody else, keep secrets, or any other tactic to avoid facing the consequences.

- Punishment chips away at the trust between a parent and child. The child no longer feels comfortable confiding in their parent due to the fear of being punished. Instead, the child might become highly agreeable, doing anything to please the parent but never exactly forming a strong bond with them.

- Punishment doesn't address the emotions that caused the child to act out in the first place, such as feeling neglected or not being emotionally validated. These emotions are left lingering inside the child and are displayed through unhealthy behaviors, which leads to more punishment and hurt feelings.

- Punishment causes a child to become self-centered, only looking out for themselves and not considering how their behaviors affect those around them.

How Discipline Works

The alternative to punishment is discipline, which is offering guidance to your child. Your role as a parent is to teach your child the difference between right and wrong behavior and provide positive reinforcement to encourage more of what you would like to see. You can think of discipline as a teachable moment where you sit down with your child and analyze their actions. Your job is to help them see why certain actions are harmful and lead to bad outcomes. Instead of instilling fear in them, you encourage them to do better next time—because you believe they can do better!

There are three important elements of effective discipline:

1. Provide Explanations for Rules

It is important for your child to understand why certain limits are necessary. Otherwise, they will blindly follow rules without feeling responsible for their behaviors. Ideally, you want your child to grow up being able to justify why they hold specific values, beliefs, and attitudes about life. This will give them the confidence to express who they are and draw boundaries with others.

Be clear about your expectations and the significance of the rules you would like them to follow. If they have questions about the rules, offer age-appropriate answers. For example, you can tell your 12-year-old daughter that TV is always watched after homework has been completed because work comes before play. If they ask why, you can explain that watching TV is a reward for hard work. This can later become a value that your child grows up with.

2. Issue Appropriate Consequences

Consequences are important, even when you are disciplining a child. They teach a child the concept of cause and effect and how every action can lead to a positive or negative outcome. Learning this lesson at a young age will teach your child the value of making good choices. With this said, the consequences should always match their behaviors. They shouldn't be too lenient or too harsh because, once again, you don't want your child's focus to be on the consequence.

If possible, consequences should be a teachable moment, an opportunity to practice the desired behavior. For example, if your toddler decides to paint on the kitchen floor tiles, you can explain why painting on the tiles is wrong, then proceed to hand them a soapy cloth and ask them to clean it up. Afterward, you can thank them and show how happy you are that they cleaned up the mess on their own. You might even say, "I am so proud of you for cleaning up your own mess. Well done!"

3. Work Together as a Team

Disciplining your child is about holding their hand through the process of understanding acceptable and unacceptable behaviors. Even though you won't prevent them from making mistakes, you are always there to support them and redirect their attention to positive behaviors. It is therefore important to communicate that you are available to help your child learn to become the best version of themselves. You might say, "Let's work together as a team to correct this mistake and learn from it."

If your child continues to repeat the same bad behaviors, see it as an opportunity to lean toward them even more. Acknowledge their feelings and ask how you can assist them. Showing your child immense love while they learn good habits will not spoil them or make them even more defiant. Instead, it will make them feel less anxious to fail and more confident to get up after every setback!

It is also important to note that, unlike punishment, discipline is not a one-off thing. After you have issued an appropriate consequence, your job is to check in with your child and find out how they are doing and if they are experiencing any of the emotions that caused their misbehavior in the first place. Sometimes, your child will need daily support to avoid certain urges or be reminded to do what is right. Eventually, they will be able to regulate their own emotions and behaviors without your daily assistance.

The Truth About the Silent Treatment

When Dominica was a child, her mother would always give her "the look" whenever she was angry with her. This was a look of disapproval that was followed by silence and a lack of eye contact. At first, Dominica used to cry whenever her mother gave her the look, but she realized that crying wouldn't get her attention. Eventually, she stopped crying for her mother's attention and became emotionally withdrawn—dealing with her strong emotions the same way her mother did.

The silent treatment, also known as stonewalling, is a tactic used to convey disapproval. After being emotionally triggered, you might feel overwhelmed and not have the words to convey what you are experiencing or need at that moment. If you have anger issues, giving the silent treatment might also be a way to manage your emotions and avoid lashing out in rage. You may so desperately want to control your own explosive emotional state that the only thing you can think of doing is checking out.

Some of the ways that you can practice the silent treatment include:

- Refusing to talk to or look at your child.

- Being indifferent to your child's existence.

- Avoiding answering questions or engaging in any form of discussion.

- Pretending that you don't notice your child trying to get your attention.

- Withholding affection and privileges and treating your child coldly.

When a child is given the silent treatment, all of the love and security they feel from their parent is taken away. This can cause a lot of confusion and frustration. They can see that their parent is no longer responsive but don't know what may have caused this reaction. Worst of all, they may blame themselves for their parent's silence and feel extremely remorseful. Out of the fear of rejection and abandonment, they might do everything in their power to avoid upsetting their parent, which of course means undermining their own physical and emotional needs.

The silent treatment falls under the emotional abuse umbrella. It is a subtle yet aggressive and damaging form of manipulation. Even though you cannot physically see the effects of this kind of abuse, your child's psychological well-being is compromised as a result of feeling temporarily abandoned and unwanted. The best way to avoid giving the silent treatment is to communicate whenever you are upset. Tell your child how their actions have hurt you and what you might need at that moment.

For instance, it is okay to take a moment for yourself to reflect on how you are feeling before engaging with your child, but let them know that you need some time alone and you will reach out to them when you are ready to talk. It is also crucial to explain that what you are feeling is not their fault and your need for space is your way of calming down—not an excuse to get away from them.

You might say, "I feel really hurt right now and I can't speak. I need 15 minutes to myself so I can calm down and feel strong enough to have a heart-to-heart with you." Notice the use of the words "I feel" and "I need." They are a reminder to your child that you are responsible for your own emotional experience.

Positive Parenting Exercise

Discipline doesn't have to be rigid, formal, and boring! There are plenty of fun activities you can do with your child to teach them self-control without applying pressure. Below are suggestions for self-discipline games that you can practice at home.

- **Play red light, green light.** Whenever you yell, "Green light!" your child needs to dance or move around, but as soon as you yell, "Red light!" they have to freeze!

- **Create a calming jar.** Grab an empty mason jar, colorful Post-it notes, and a pen. Sit down with your child and write down positive coping strategies to manage stress and anxiety. Leave the jar in their room, and whenever they are upset, encourage them to open their jar and grab a note.

- **Create a safe space at home.** Find a snug corner that you and your child can turn into a safe space. This is where they will retreat whenever they need to calm down and collect their thoughts. It's important to make this space look exceptionally beautiful, according to your child's preferences. If you have an older child, consider revamping the garden shed or cottage into their safe space and help them decorate it with their favorite items.

- **Reflect on the rose, thorn, and bud of the day.** Encourage your child to share their thoughts and emotions by asking them to reflect on the highs and lows of their day. The rose represents their small wins, the thorns are the challenges, and the bud is the things they are looking forward to.

Chapter 7:

Age-Appropriate

Communication With Kids

Children have never been very good at listening to their elders, but they have never failed to imitate them. –James Baldwin

How You Talk Matters

As a parent, you spend a lot of time considering what kinds of values, behaviors, and life lessons you want to teach your child. You are aware that, as your child gets older and gains more independence, imparting these messages to them won't always be easy. However, when a child is listening to you speak, they are not necessarily paying attention to what you say but rather how your message comes across.

Regardless of how good your intentions are, when you speak to your child in a manner that comes across aggressively, they will not be able to hear and respect what you are saying. Instead of learning from your words, they are left feeling wounded by how you made them feel.

Communication skills are essential in any type of relationship. Just think about it: Two unique individuals, holding different social or economic positions, come together to exchange ideas with each other and hope to develop a strong bond. Without the ability to articulate thoughts in a manner that is simplest for each person to understand and interpret correctly, there are bound to be misunderstandings.

But beyond articulation, effective communication requires empathy and social awareness. Before you can share a message, you must be able to adjust the tone, language, and delivery for the specific individual you are speaking to. For instance, you might want to express how overwhelmed you are feeling, but depending on who you are speaking to—whether it is your boss, spouse, or a random stranger—how you convey that message will look and feel different.

A child is naturally sensitive to the words spoken by their parents. This has to do with their dependency on the parent-child relationship for safety and reassurance. Hearing their parent speak in a warm, loving tone reassures the child of their parent's affection. It doesn't really matter what is said (if they were given a compliment or discipline), the child walks away feeling secure about their parent-child relationship.

In contrast, hearing parents speak in a critical or condescending tone can trigger a child's natural defenses and put them on edge. This type of aggressive communication threatens their sense of safety and compromises the parent-child bond. Without a sense of safety, the child is left feeling powerless in the relationship and confused about how to relate to or connect with their parent moving forward.

Affirming a child isn't only in what you say, like reminding them of how much you love them. It is also expressed by how you communicate. Put yourself in your child's shoes for a moment and think about how they felt about themselves and their relationship with you the last time you were in an argument. During the argument, do you think they felt loved or judged? Supported or condemned? And what exactly do you think caused them to feel that way? Was it the message you communicated, the way you delivered the message, or both?

In this chapter, we will explore different ways to communicate with kids in a manner that can strengthen the parent-child relationship. The focus here will not be so much on choosing the right words but more on delivering messages (whether you are praising your child or disciplining them) in a way that boosts their self-confidence and makes them feel cherished.

Seven Verbal and Nonverbal Communication Tips for Positive Interactions

Your child is obligated to listen to you because of the power dynamics in your relationship. But just because your child is listening to you doesn't mean they respect what you are saying or that they have been positively influenced by it. For example, your child may listen to you because they fear confrontation or punishment. In this case, what you say to them doesn't have the power to positively change their behaviors because they aren't inspired to act differently.

To improve the way you communicate with your child, it is important to learn what positive communication looks and sounds like. Before doing that, you need to understand the different types of communication available to you. Communication can be separated into two categories: verbal and nonverbal. Verbal communication is messages that are delivered in spoken words. There are three factors that enhance your verbal communication:

- the pitch and tone of your voice

- the kinds of words spoken

- dialect, or making use of simple, child-friendly language

There is also nonverbal communication, which are messages delivered without any words spoken. Instead of words, body language, gestures, physical touch, and facial expressions are used to convey information.

There are right and wrong ways of using verbal and nonverbal communication. For example, speaking in a judgmental tone, saying hurtful words, or using mature language with a young child will most likely reduce the effectiveness of your message, as will avoiding eye contact, crossing your arms, or displaying a look of contempt. However, if you speak with compassion, utter encouraging words, and use age-appropriate language, you can successfully get your message across to them.

Below are seven verbal and nonverbal communication tips that will improve how you share messages with your child—and subsequently influence their positive behaviors.

1. Consider Your Intention

Before speaking to your child, take a moment to consider the intention behind your message. Ask yourself, "What do I want to say?" Those few seconds spent on formulating an intentional message can prevent impulsive utterances that you later regret.

2. Use Age-Appropriate Language

In order for your message to be clear, your child must be able to understand what you are saying—and interpret the message accordingly. This means using words that are simple enough for them to understand, depending on their age. Remember that your message should make your child feel loved and respected rather than patronized or undermined.

3. Practice Active Listening

An effective communicator is also a good listener. If you want to convey messages that touch your child's heart and trigger positive change, you will need to spend time listening to them share their thoughts and feelings. Listening to your child without the intention to respond or provide a counterargument makes them feel respected. As a result, they are more likely to show you the same courtesy and value what you have to say.

4. Avoid Making Threats

When there is a sense of openness and comfortability between you and your child, communication flows and both of you feel confident expressing your views, even when you disagree. Making threats and using other forms of violent verbal and nonverbal communication causes distrust and restricts the flow of communication. Sit down with your child and create clear communication expectations, writing down acceptable and unacceptable words, attitudes, and behaviors when speaking to each other. Hold each other accountable to these expectations.

5. Practice Reflective Listening

Reflective listening is another type of listening that allows you to empathize with your child's experience and show them that you care. It involves repeating back what you heard them say using different words and asking for clarity. For example, if your child says, "You never listen to me!" you can respond, "You don't feel like I listen to you?" This creates space for your child to open up even more and share their emotional experience without feeling scared or judged. Be sure your tone is gentle rather than sarcastic or mocking.

6. Explain What You Are Noticing

Whether you are praising your child for good behavior, providing feedback on ways they can improve, or correcting bad behavior, always begin by sharing what you are noticing. When you do this, you are giving your child an opportunity to reflect on their behaviors too and learn the difference between acceptable and unacceptable behavior. This means that instead of saying, "Thank you for cleaning your room," you can say, "I noticed that you vacuumed your carpet. It looks really good. Nice work!"

7. Focus on the Behavior, Not the Person

You are allowed to feel upset about your child's bad attitudes or behaviors. However, when showing disapproval, make sure that you focus on their actions rather than on them as a person. Your child did a bad thing, but they are not a bad person. Together, you can have a heartfelt conversation about the behavior in question without turning the conversation personal. It may even be necessary to remind your child during the conversation that you are against their bad behavior but still love them unconditionally.

It is worth emphasizing again that you are allowed to be angry and display strong emotions when you are upset. However, feeling angry doesn't have to lead to harsh or disrespectful communication. By communicating with purpose, being clear about your message, explaining what you are noticing, and focusing on the troublesome behavior rather than attacking your child, you can have a productive conversation that leads to a positive resolution.

Communication strategies tend to vary when speaking to children of different ages. What gets the message across to a four-year-old won't necessarily work for a 14-year-old. The following sections will explore the key factors for communicating with toddlers, young children, and teenagers.

The Secret for Communicating With Toddlers: Empathy

Getting a toddler to listen or follow instructions can be a challenge for even the most patient parents. You might raise your voice, give "the look," or even make threats, and your toddler will remain in the same spot, flashing the biggest smile. Many frustrated parents will nag or repeat the same message over and over again until they eventually lose their temper.

The best way to get a toddler to cooperate is to teach them how to behave and help them learn how to express their emotions. This can be done by teaching and modeling empathy.

Empathy is the ability to understand another person's perspective and respond with compassion. When your toddler develops empathy, they are able to see themselves as an individual separate from others and as having different thoughts and feelings than others too. They can look at a situation and imagine how the next person might feel at that moment and instinctively seek ways of comforting them.

Communicating with your child becomes a lot easier once they develop some degree of empathy because they are able to imagine the impact of their behavior on those around them. For example, before a work meeting, you might say to your child, "Mommy is getting on a phone call with her big boss. If Mommy can't hear her boss, they will get upset. Can you please help Mommy by playing quietly and not making noise?"

From this request, your toddler can imagine the serious nature of this phone call because the "big boss" is painted out to be some kind of authoritarian figure who holds more power than Mommy. They can also understand the impact of making noise and how that would place Mommy in an awkward position— which, of course, they don't want to do.

Teaching your child empathy begins at an early age—as early as six months old. At that stage of development, your child learns what is known as social referencing—or copycatting. They will observe your body language and mannerisms in social situations to figure out the most appropriate ways to behave. Displaying empathy, such as showing concern for others, can teach your child to do the same.

Between 18–24 months of age, your child will start to develop their own ideas and thoughts, which may or may not be similar to yours. At this stage, they begin to entertain their own ideas of good and bad behavior. They may even test their assumptions of good and bad behavior by performing certain actions in front of you and seeing how you react. Responding empathetically to your child, such as by validating their emotions, teaches them that sharing their thoughts and feelings is good. This will later help them develop more tolerance for others.

Empathy must be continually taught in order for it to become the standard way of communication. Below are suggestions on how you can teach your toddler how to be more empathetic.

1. Validate Your Toddler's Strong Emotions

Instead of going into problem-solving mode when your child is sad or frustrated, create a safe space for them to feel and process the pain. Reassure them that being upset is normal and they will get through it. You can even help them cope better with their feelings by labeling their emotion. You might say, "You are angry that you can't play outside. I understand. You love playing with your ball in the yard."

2. Teach Empathy Through Role-Playing

While role-playing with your child, create scenarios where empathy would be shown. For example, you might be a sick patient in a hospital and your toddler is the doctor taking care of you. Or maybe you are a crying baby and your child is the mother or father who calms you down. After your child has demonstrated empathy, you can praise them for how they handled the situation.

3. Focus on the Other Person's Feelings

Most of the time when a child misbehaves, we are quick to tell them to apologize for what they have done. However, a toddler doesn't fully understand the meaning behind the words "I am sorry," nor can they connect the phrase with their bad behavior. Instead of getting your child to apologize, teach them how to observe another person's feelings. This way, they can easily connect their behaviors (good or bad) with a person's emotional reaction.

For example, you might flip through a magazine and look at images of adults and children. You can point out various facial expressions and gestures and explain what they mean. You can then ask your child what they think might have happened to cause that emotional reaction.

4. Teach Your Toddler Self-Care

Sometimes, toddlers show a lack of empathy, not because they don't know how, but because they are overwhelmed by their own strong emotions. It is therefore important to teach them how to respond to their emotional needs and self-regulate so that they can be more aware of the needs of others. A simple breathing technique, like taking a deep breath and counting to five then breathing out, can prevent an emotional outburst and help your child release tension.

5. Practice How to Resolve Conflicts

Conflicts are a natural part of relationships. Talking and role-playing about resolving conflicts can improve how you and your child solve problems and engage in tough conversations.

There are various age-appropriate conflict resolution skills you can practice with your toddler, such as listening when someone else is speaking, paraphrasing what you have heard, giving each other space to calm down, and showing acceptance for the other person's feelings.

You can also teach your child how to view conflicts. For instance, you can reframe conflicts from being a "parent versus child" situation to being a "parent and child versus the problem" situation. When initiating a tough conversation, you can start by saying, "We have a problem that we need to solve together."

Empathy is a valuable communication skill that will teach your toddler how to relate to other people in a healthy manner. They will learn that what they think or feel isn't necessarily how another person thinks or feels. The ability to hold space for others and show concern for their feelings will also make it easier for your child to understand the impact of their behaviors on others. When you are upset with them, they can imagine how their actions have hurt your feelings.

The Secret for Communicating With Young Children: Validation

When your child gets older, they start to develop a sense of self. They are curious about the world and the role they play in it. Communicating with your child requires more than just showing and practicing empathy. They need you to validate their thoughts and feelings and show acceptance for the person they are becoming.

As was mentioned early in Chapter 1, validation is about letting your child know that you understand them. You may not agree with everything they say or do, but that doesn't take away from the love and support you show them. When your child feels heard, they are able to let their guard down, accept their emotions, and feel comfortable in their own skin. This helps them maintain healthy boundaries with others and develop a positive self-image.

Every parent desires a confident and self-regulated child. However, in order for them to figure out who they are and gain self-confidence, young children will often engage in power struggles with their parents. A power struggle occurs when a parent gives an instruction and the child refuses to follow it. The parent might insist that the child act immediately, and the child might drag their feet or challenge the request. This battle of wills leaves the parent feeling angry and desperate and the child feeling unheard. No one ever wins a power struggle.

Understanding why power struggles happen in the first place can defuse them. Young children want to be validated by their parents because that's what makes them feel seen and heard in the relationship. Communicating with a young child without validating them causes defensive behavior. They feel almost cornered and forced to show their parents that they can stand up for themselves. In most cases, it wasn't the instruction that upset the child, but rather feeling as though their parents are not considerate of their feelings.

Ending power struggles begins by connecting with your child. This could be as simple as spending time with them and listening to what they have going on in their life. Ask your child questions about school, their friendships, or what they are looking forward to. You can even engage in playful activities that allow you to bond without getting involved in serious conversations.

Once you have established a strong bond with your child, the next important step is to demonstrate trust by backing off. This doesn't mean going completely off the radar or giving them too much space or choice; instead, it means playing a supportive role in their life. If they are curious about trying a new activity, let them try it out and gain that experience. When it comes to their household chores, let them decide how to complete the tasks rather than telling them what to do.

A growing child who is exploring who they are wants to gain a sense of control. Even though they know that their parents are responsible for taking care of them, they desire to have some control over their life. This is what makes them feel validated by their parents and accepted for who they are. Below are a few strategies for how you can validate your child and make them feel powerful.

1. Acknowledge Your Child's Feelings

You and your child might look at the same situation and walk away feeling differently about it. Neither of your perspectives is wrong, they just prove that how something affects you may not always affect your child the same way. Acknowledging your child's feelings validates their emotional experience. It gives your child permission to feel however they choose to feel about a situation without feeling guilty.

Showing acknowledgment can be as simple as saying, "I know this situation is stressful for you," or, "I can imagine how difficult it is to hear that." The aim isn't to try and change or fix how they feel but to be present in the experience with them.

2. Delay Giving Correction

When your child is acting out, don't be quick to assume their intentions. Have an open conversation and allow them to share their thoughts and feelings before handing out corrections.

What matters most is making your child feel seen and heard rather than judged for their behavior. Your child is more likely to cooperate with you when they sense your concern and desire to understand where they are coming from.

3. Give Choices, Not Orders

Giving your child options can be a great way to empower them and defuse a power struggle. Have a goal in mind and create three choices that your child can choose from to accomplish the goal. For example, you might lay out three different outfits on the bed and let them choose their favorite one, or describe three household chores and ask them to choose which one they would like to handle.

When deciding on the choices, make sure that they are not too rigid. For example, saying to your child, "Either you watch this movie or you go to sleep," doesn't give them much of a choice. The better approach would be saying, "You have three choices of which movie to watch." This at least gives them enough wiggle room to decide on what movie they are most interested in rather than being forced to watch a specific movie.

4. Accept Your Child's "No"

Parents tend to get uncomfortable when hearing "no" from their children. Some look at it as a sign of disrespect rather than as a boundary being drawn. What is interesting, though, is that parents are quick to say no to their children sometimes without even providing an explanation. To validate your child's experiences, you will need to learn to respect their boundaries. There are some thoughts or feelings they may not want to share with you or certain activities they may feel uncomfortable performing. Accept their decisions and what that might mean for you (i.e., not getting what you want). Realize that these boundaries will help them form secure relationships later in life.

5. Make Your Child Feel Powerful

If you want to raise a secure, confident, and self-respecting child, it is crucial that you make them feel powerful. What this means is praising good behaviors, offering encouragement, assigning special tasks or responsibilities for them to do, valuing what they have to say, and showing them respect. A child who feels powerless will seek control using any means possible—even if it means performing acts of sabotage and becoming rebellious. Your child shouldn't have to misbehave to get your attention.

Your child wants to know that they are a good person and make positive contributions to the family and their community. This positive sense of self is what shapes who they become and their willingness to express themselves in other relationships. Validating your child won't spoil them. It will help them find their voice, set healthy boundaries, identify and manage their emotions, and feel empowered in their relationships.

The Secret for Communicating With Teenagers: Respect

The transition from young child to teenager requires another adjustment to how you communicate with your child. While empathy and validation are still important, showing respect is what keeps the lines of communication open and maintains a strong foundation of trust in your relationship.

If you are raising a teenager, you know how difficult it can be to get through to them. They are no longer as cooperative as they used to be, and they may continue the power struggles. This noncooperative and combative approach is often interpreted as disrespect. You may feel hopeless in finding the best ways to parent your child because your authority as a parent is constantly challenged.

Like any frustrated parent, you may be tempted to increase the severity of your discipline, withdraw certain privileges, and enforce arbitrary rules to demonstrate that you are still in control. But how effective are these strategies in influencing your teen's behaviors? Do they become more cooperative and respectful? The answer is no. In fact, playing up your power only creates distance between you and your child, making it harder to bond.

To get through to your teenager, you will need to show respect before expecting respect. This might require a mindset shift. For instance, when your child is ignoring you, the first question you ought to ask yourself is, "How much respect have I displayed up until this point?" and consider how that might have influenced their behavior.

Teenagers have a need to feel respected due to their increasing desire for autonomy. They are aware that, in a few years, they will become adults, so their adolescent years are spent unconsciously preparing for adulthood. Micromanaging your teenager or placing too many restrictions on their freedoms will only make them revolt and seek to demonstrate their independence, even if it means becoming rebellious.

Teenagers are hypersensitive to the amount of autonomy they are given by their parents. When they feel coerced, smothered, or controlled, it will trigger what is known as an autonomy threat. You will notice that your child's stress levels have increased and they are either more aggressive or flighty. Moreover, they adopt maladaptive coping strategies to deal with the stress, which may include shutting down emotionally, a lack of cooperation, and more childish behaviors.

Researchers and scientists who have investigated teenage rebellion believe that part of what causes a teenager to act out is having their autonomy threatened. For example, studies have shown that teenagers were more willing to cooperate with parents when they believed that the rules enforced were fair, but they resisted when they saw the rules as being opinion-based or unjust.

How parents talk with teenagers has also been found to trigger an autonomy threat. Criticizing, for example, has been found to cause teenagers to shut down. Neuroscientists observed that when a parent utters a critical statement, the regions of the brain associated with emotional regulation and social cognition show less activity. This means that teenagers are not able to respond appropriately to their parents when they feel like they are being criticized.

The key to effective communication with teenagers is to find ways to share messages without violating your child's need for respect and autonomy. This doesn't mean that you can't discipline your child, but you must be mindful of how your approach to discipline makes your child feel. Below are a few strategies for how to communicate respectfully with your teenager.

1. Show Understanding

Modern teenagers are faced with unique challenges that previous generations have never had to deal with. You won't always relate to your child or share the same beliefs and opinions as them, but it is important to show understanding nonetheless. Put yourself in their shoes and consider the kinds of things that may take priority in their life. Try to imagine the significance of the phase they are in and what they need from you as a parent.

For example, staying connected might be one of your child's top priorities. In order to stay connected, they spend a lot of time on social media. As a parent, you understand the dangers of social media and aren't comfortable with your child's dependency on it. However, if you step into their shoes, you will realize that the best way to show love and respect for your child is to advise them on how to stay safe online and take a step back so you can play a supportive role.

You can say to your child, "I understand how important it is for you to stay connected with your friends. If I am being honest, I feel scared about how frequently you go online. I want to rest assured that you are safe while engaging on social media. Can we have an open discussion about safety measures online?"

2. Don't Take Everything Personally

It can be hurtful to receive an eye roll, deep sighs, or the silent treatment from your child. You are reminded of the sweet, innocent angel they used to be and feel angry that your relationship has changed so drastically. However, looking at your child's behaviors from an emotional perspective will only make you feel worse about yourself as a parent.

Remind yourself that your teenager is a unique individual whose decisions are not a reflection of you. They choose to behave in certain ways based on their ideas of what is acceptable and unacceptable. The truth is your child may not have the necessary skills to make good choices or regulate their emotions. The best you can do is guide them toward making good choices. Your emotional availability and unconditional love will reassure your child that they are capable of being the best version of themselves.

3. Engage Your Child With Questions

Replace telling your teenager what to do with asking them insightful questions that get them thinking. By doing this, you are placing the decision-making power in your child's hands and showing how much you trust them.

For example, if you know that it is your child's turn to wash dishes, instead of saying, "Don't forget to wash the dishes," you would say, "Whose turn is it to wash the dishes today?" You can also ask your child questions about how they plan on solving problems. For example, you might say, "You have an exam coming up on Monday. How is your study timetable looking?" Or if you notice that your child is constantly waking up late, you might ask, "Do you have any ideas for how you can get up on time?"

Make sure that your child knows that you are there to help them solve problems but won't micromanage them. It is important to let them make some big decisions during their teen years because you are preparing them for adulthood where they will have to take full responsibility for their choices.

4. Don't Expect Good Behavior

When you make it obvious that you expect your teenager to behave a certain way, you may trigger an autonomy threat. Your child wants to feel like their behaviors are a result of their choices, not your expectations. Even though you desire cooperation from your child, you cannot expect it from them. Instead of creating expectations, practice accepting your child as they are. Realize that they are human and will make plenty of mistakes as they learn how to become independent. Tell yourself that, regardless of how your child acts, your openness and affection toward them will remain constant. In other words, no matter what choices they make, you will still love them.

Please note that dropping expectations of good behavior doesn't mean dropping boundaries. If your child violates a boundary, they will face the same consequences. You will continue to hold them accountable to the standards you have enforced at home; however, whether they wake up in a good or bad mood is not something you need to be overly concerned about.

5. Avoid Engaging With Your Child Before You Are Calm

It is never a good idea to engage in a conversation with your child when either of you is upset. Both of you are more likely to say things that you don't mean when you are emotional. It is okay to take time for yourself and check in with your feelings before enforcing discipline. Process how you are feeling and what your needs are, and encourage your child to do the same. Remember, the purpose of conflict resolution is to find a solution to a problem.

Parenting your child won't look the same at every age. As your child grows, their needs will look different. For instance, your toddler wants to be assured that it is safe to express their feelings. When they become a young child, they want you to accept them for who they are. As a teenager, what matters most is knowing that you trust them to make decisions affecting their life. Adapting to their communication needs can reduce misunderstandings and ensure that you maintain a strong bond with your child.

Positive Parenting Exercise

Place a number of obstacles in a room and a prize hidden somewhere among them. Blindfold your child and direct them through the obstacles to locate the prize. Once your child has found the prize, it is their turn to hide another prize, reorganize the obstacles, and blindfold you. This game is designed to encourage cooperation and active listening as well as to build trust between you and your child.

Chapter 8:

What You Need to Know About Positive Parenting

Behind every young child who believes in himself is a parent who believed first. –Matthew Jacobson

What Is Positive Parenting?

We cannot speak about anger management for parents without touching on parenting styles. A parenting style is a philosophy that informs your approach to parenting. Every parent has a parenting style whether they are aware of it or not.

For example, a family might practice authoritarian parenting, which creates high expectations for children to follow with little positive reinforcement. Another family might practice uninvolved parenting where children are left to their own devices most of the time and parents show little responsiveness. As you can tell, every parenting approach comes with its own set of behaviors and customs, which in turn impact the behaviors of the children involved.

Positive parenting is a relatively new parenting style that provides an alternative to aggressive forms of parenting that include things like exerting control, showing hostility, shaming, and withdrawing affection. It is based on showing empathy by offering encouragement and taking a collaborative approach to problem-solving.

Parents who use positive parenting are proactive in responding to their children's needs through positive interactions. This is the main strategy that they believe can prevent bad behaviors from occurring in the first place. The idea is that the more emotionally present and responsive a parent is, the more secure the child will feel.

So, what exactly does positive parenting look like in practice? In summary, positive parenting is about:

- Spending one-on-one time with your child and being present during moments of bonding.

- Recognizing and praising specific behaviors with affirmative words and physical touch.

- Being compassionate with yourself as a parent and focusing on the things within your control.

- Being consistent with setting healthy boundaries and enforcing age-appropriate consequences.

- Using positive interactions with your child to model good behavior and correct troublesome behaviors.

- Striking a balance between responding to your needs as well as your child's needs.

Positive Parenting vs. Other Parenting Styles

Cindy went to the supermarket with her five-year-old son, Mark. Before they got out of the car, Cindy made an agreement with him that they were going inside the store to buy bread, milk, and tomatoes. If he was well-behaved—which meant staying close to his mother and not picking up any items—he could pick an ice cream of his choice on the way out.

Both of them agreed to the plan, but a few minutes after entering the supermarket, all bets were off! Her son was going in between aisles, grabbing items, and placing them inside the basket. Cindy gave her son two warnings about his behavior:

"Mark, you are not walking close to me or keeping your hands to yourself like we agreed in the car. If you continue to pick up items, we are not going to get ice cream on the way out."

Mark seemed to understand the seriousness of the warnings, but not enough to get him to actually listen. For the remainder of the shopping trip, Cindy's goal was to monitor her son's behaviors so that he wouldn't hurt himself or break anything. But in her mind, she knew that a consequence would need to be enforced very soon.

When they got to the checkout stand, Mark asked about the reward of ice cream. Cindy responded by explaining the agreement once more and how Mark's actions meant the deal was off. He began to cry, and she went down on one knee to his level to comfort him.

"You're angry that you can't get an ice cream, aren't you?" she asked. He responded with a tearful nod. "How about next time we practice walking in the supermarket together so that you can walk away with an ice cream?" He nodded once more and dried his tears. The consequence was bitter, but a lesson was learned: Mommy clearly meant business when she said to stay close while shopping.

Positive parenting is often criticized as being passive, but that is far from the truth. Yes, it is true that with positive parenting, there is no tolerance for punishment, like shouting, spanking, grounding, or traditional time-outs. However, positive discipline is still carried out through teaching and reinforcing values and boundaries. There are two other common styles of parenting besides positive parenting: authoritarian and permissive.

Authoritarian parenting is strict and tends to force expectations on a child. The child is told to act a certain way simply because the parent said so or because that's how it has always been done in the family. The parent behaves like an authority figure, preferring to lecture rather than mentor their child, and any deviations from their rules are met with threats or punishment. A child raised in this kind of environment does act obediently, but that doesn't mean they are positively influenced by their parents. In fact, they are more likely to struggle with sharing their thoughts and emotions or trusting their own decision-making abilities when they grow up.

Permissive parenting, on the other hand, promotes indulgence and freedom. A child is given free rein to act as they wish with very few consequences for bad behavior. Parents who use this approach avoid confrontation at all costs because they don't want to upset their child. Boundaries are seen as oppressive and unloving, so the child isn't raised with the necessary structure that allows them to build a healthy sense of self and learn the difference between acceptable and unacceptable behaviors. The lack of discipline harms the child in the long run, especially when they get older and begin to find their own feet.

Positive parenting takes aspects of authoritarian and permissive parenting and creates a parenting approach that is liberal yet structured and predictable. The child is raised being taught that their needs matter, and an open line of communication is established between them and their parents from an early age. Unlike permissive parenting, the child isn't given free will to decide on their behaviors. There are clear rules and expectations reinforced through positive and loving interactions. Parents won't force their child to follow the rules but instead encourage cooperation by building trust, validating the child's experiences, and respecting their viewpoints.

There is one factor that distinguishes positive parenting from the other parenting approaches: The emphasis on teaching. Parents who adopt the positive parenting style are present and proactive in teaching their child how to navigate life and make good choices. They become their child's mentor and coach, helping them identify problematic behaviors, adjust their perspectives, and develop positive habits and coping strategies. They do still set boundaries and enforce consequences, but the child is taught the significance of boundaries and the purpose behind the consequence. In other words, even discipline is seen as a teachable moment to help the child understand cause and effect.

In comparison to the other parenting styles, positive parenting does require a lot more commitment from parents. But parents can think of it as an investment they are making to raise a child who has a strong internal locus of control and who is confident enough to embrace the challenges of life, learn from their mistakes, and develop healthy relationships built on mutual respect and healthy boundaries.

Six Positive Parenting Strategies

Positive parenting isn't about being relaxed when you need to be firm or allowing your child to get away with bad behaviors. It is all about holding your child accountable to age-appropriate rules and expectations. However, there is a certain way that your child is held accountable without harming their self-esteem. This is done through positive interactions that support your child's well-being and reinforce your unconditional love.

There are many different positive parenting strategies that you can use to enforce positive discipline and strengthen your relationship with your child. What is common about these strategies is that they focus on nurturing good behavior rather than punishing bad behavior. Below are six strategies that you can practice with your toddler, young child, and teenager at home.

1. Practice Being Present

Being present in the moment is about paying attention to what is happening around you. At home, it can look like spending uninterrupted time with your child, engaging in a game that you play together, or watching a movie (if you have an older child). Your presence makes your child feel safe and protected. When spending time with you becomes a norm, they may even confide in you when they are going through a difficult time.

Toddler tip: When playing with your toddler, say a word related to the toy and ask them to repeat it after you. For example, your toddler might be pushing a yellow truck and you can say, "Truck. Say 'truck,' Hannah. Truck."

Young child tip: Start a project with your child that requires at least three sessions to complete. Before each session, set a goal and work toward accomplishing it together. Praise them for their efforts and reflect on your progress.

Teenager tip: Take your teenager out on a "date" to one of their favorite places. Make sure that there aren't too many distractions around so you have an opportunity to chat. Show an interest in their life and ask open-ended questions like "What's been happening in your friendship circle?"

2. Be a Role Model

Your child learns more from watching your actions than from hearing you speak. If you want to instill certain values in your child, pay attention to how you behave around them. Imagine that your child is watching how you react in every social situation and taking note of the choices you make. It might help to go on your own personal growth journey so you can continue improving your habits and general approach to life.

Toddler tip: When you notice that you are emotionally triggered, take a moment to yourself and practice healthy coping techniques to calm down.

Young child tip: When making certain decisions at home, talk about them with your child and explain the significance behind them. You can also offer age-appropriate explanations for family values, rules, and boundaries.

Teenager tip: Open up to your teenager about some of the challenges you faced in your adolescence. Share your experiences and how you dealt with stressful situations, but be mindful not to overshare. This will allow them to see your human side and feel inspired to conquer their own challenges.

3. Set Positive Boundaries

Boundaries don't need to be associated with harsh rules and punishment. In your household, boundaries can become synonymous with learning and growth. The reason you set boundaries is to teach your child valuable lessons about life and assist them in becoming the best version of themself. Present boundaries in a positive way, explaining the value behind them and how they can lead to positive life outcomes.

Toddler tip: When reprimanding your child, avoid using restrictive words like "no" or "can't." For example, instead of saying, "No yelling while I'm on the phone," you can say, "Please use your small voice while I'm on the phone."

Young child tip: Choose five behaviors that are most important for your child to display at home. Create house rules based on these five behaviors (developing an acronym can make learning the rules easier). Focus on redirecting your child to these behaviors rather than putting a spotlight on bad behaviors. For example, if your child yells at their younger sibling, you can remind them about the importance of being kind.

Teenager tip: Help your teenager come up with their own schedule and task lists so they can learn how to manage their time and set priorities. Work together to create a good school-life balance and dedicate enough time for rest, social activities, and working toward their goals.

4. Find the Problem Behind the Behavior

There is more to your child's problematic behaviors than what you see. In most cases, what motivates your child to act out is a result of not having their needs met. Your goal as a parent should be to sit down with your child and have an open conversation about how they are doing and explore their concerns. There may be internal and external factors that are causing your child to display the behavior, such as recent family conflict, school events, friendship breakdowns, personal insecurities, and more.

Toddler tip: Start to notice patterns behind your toddler's behavior, like what kinds of situations make them cry, irritable, or restless. Try to avoid these triggers or at least make preparations in advance to regulate your child's behavior when they get upset.

Young child tip: Instead of jumping at the opportunity to discipline your child, ask them questions about the motivation behind their problematic behavior. For instance, you might ask, "Why did you feel the need to throw your toys?" From their response, you can dig deeper, asking more "why" questions, until you get down to the root of their behavior—which will generally highlight an emotional need.

Teenager tip: To help your teenager improve how they express themselves, encourage them to start journaling. When they are feeling stressed or overwhelmed, they can log their emotional experience in a notebook. Eventually, they will be able to reflect on their experiences and identify patterns of thinking or recurring strong emotions that you can help them address.

5. Turn Mistakes Into Teachable Moments

When your child makes a mistake, you can treat it as an opportunity to reinforce core values and good habits. In other words, the learning never stops, even when your child hits a roadblock. There are so many lessons that can be learned from making mistakes, such as taking accountability, problem-solving, making good choices, and being considerate of others. You can also use it as a moment for storytelling and drawing on your own childhood experiences.

Toddler tip: When your toddler misbehaves, show them how desirable the outcomes of good behaviors are. For instance, if your child hits another child, you can show them how much more satisfying it is to share toys and play together.

Young child tip: When your child is upset, help them think of three coping strategies they can practice to calm down and feel better about themselves. Give them some space to practice the strategies they choose, then check back to see how they are feeling and what they learned from the experience.

Teenager tip: Help your teenager create a stress-management plan before difficult situations. Go through the possible scenarios and brainstorm possible solutions together. You can also create a list of potential triggers and relaxing techniques they can practice on the spot.

6. Use Positive Reinforcement

It is crucial to stop and acknowledge the positive things your child does. Highlighting what is good and overlooking what is bad builds self-confidence and promotes good behaviors. In other words, your child is motivated to behave well because they see how rewarding it is to follow rules and expectations.

Toddler tip: Show your toddler attention when they perform good behavior and limit your attention when they misbehave.

Young child tip: Be vocal about your child's strengths, talents, and skills. Tell them how great they are at helping others, doing math, or playing football. Encourage them to continue improving in these areas by providing the necessary support. For example, if your child loves taking care of animals, go with them to visit a shelter once a month, or if they are really good at math, consider getting a math tutor who can challenge them to get even better.

Teenager tip: Allow your teenager to choose from a list of privileges whenever they perform good behavior. To make the privileges more enticing, let them control what they put on the list. You can rank the privileges according to the kinds of behaviors exhibited. For instance, exceptional behaviors earn them exceptional rewards—this also reinforces the value of hard work.

Positive Parenting Exercise

The traditional time-out is seen as an effective consequence for bad behavior. However, more psychologists are discovering that isolating your child from others and withdrawing affection can actually feel more like a punishment to a child than a teachable moment.

Instead of creating separation when your child has done something wrong, try leaning toward them by practicing a "time-in." Find a quiet place where you can sit together while they calm down. Hold them in a loving embrace and say reassuring phrases like, "Everything will be okay," "I am here with you," and "You are safe." Once your child has calmed down, discuss their bad behavior and how it hurts them and those around them. End the time-in by explaining the importance of consequences, then enforce an age-appropriate consequence.

Conclusion

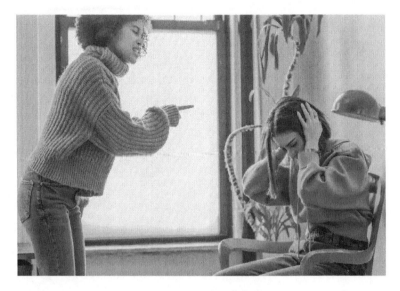

There are many parents who carry unresolved emotional wounds from their early life experiences. These wounds, coupled with everyday life stressors and parenting responsibilities, are enough to make them explode in anger. But unfortunately, when they unleash their rage, particularly on their children, what we see is a ruthless tyrant rather than years of lingering trauma and pain.

Being a parent is a role that a person takes on. However, before they become parents, they are ordinary people facing the same life challenges as anyone else. Their patterns of behavior and emotional history aren't somehow erased as soon as they bring a human being into the world. They are carried over into the new parenting role and affect the parent-child relationship.

The purpose of this book is to expose a pattern of behavior that can damage the bond between a parent and their child. This pattern of behavior is known as anger issues. It is important not to confuse being angry with having anger issues. Anger is a natural defense that arises when you feel threatened. It causes you to react aggressively as a way to protect yourself from perceived threats. However, once the threat is gone, the anger should also subside.

Having a low tolerance for distress, lashing out in uncontrollable rage, and seeking ways to hurt others when you are upset are signs of anger issues. Your reaction is much bigger and more intense than the offense, and the trigger may not even have to do with what is taking place here and now. The reason anger issues must be identified and dealt with is that they create dysfunctional family dynamics, negatively affecting how family members relate to and communicate with one another.

Behind anger issues are deep-rooted psychological problems that more than likely stem from childhood as a result of how you were raised and the harmful coping strategies you adopted as a result. Addressing these issues requires taking a trip down memory lane, identifying unresolved trauma, and working through unconscious beliefs, impulsive behaviors, and emotional triggers that have dictated how you relate to people in your adult relationships.

All of this work will be worth it when you can finally enjoy the role of parenting your child and provide them with all the security and affection you may not have received when you were growing up.

Managing your anger is the first step to positive parenting and learning how to be a positive role model for your child. Your ability to take care of your well-being, set healthy personal boundaries, and adopt healthy habits can positively influence your child.

Whether you are aware of it or not, your child is constantly observing how you face life's challenges to decide on how they should approach life too. Therefore, working through your own struggles and becoming the best version of yourself is the best gift you can ever give your child!

A Message from the Author

If you enjoyed the book and are interested on further updates or just a place to share your thoughts, please join **https://www.facebook.com/groups/richard.bass.author or scan.**

If you would be interested on receiving a FREE ADHD Planner for kids PDF version, by signing up you will also receive exclusive notifications to when new content is released and will be able to receive it at a promotional price. Scan below for email sign up!

Check out my YouTube page for more tips and explanations on Neuro-development.

About the Author

Richard Bass is a well-established author with extensive knowledge and background on children's disabilities. He is the author of A Beginner's Guide on Parenting Children with ADHD, Parenting Children with Oppositional Defiant Disorder, Parenting a Child with Autism, Overcoming Anxiety and Depression in Teens and The Effective Anger Management Guide for Parents. He has also experienced firsthand many children and teens who deal with depression and anxiety. Richard also enjoys researching techniques and ideas to better serve students as well as providing guidance to parents on how to understand and lead their children to success.

Richard wants to share his experience, research, and practices through his writing as it has proven successful for many parents and students. He feels there is a need for parents and others around the child to fully understand the disability or mental health of the child. He hopes that with his writing, people will be more understanding of children going through these issues.

In regards to his qualifications, Richard holds a bachelor's and master's degree in education as well as several certifications including Special Education K-12 and Educational Administration. Whenever he is not working, reading, or writing, he likes to travel with his family to learn about different cultures as well as get ideas from all around about the upbringing of children, especially those with disabilities. He also researches and learns about different educational systems around the world.

Richard participates in several online groups where parents, educators, doctors, and psychologists share their successes with children with disabilities. He also has his own group where further discussion about his books and techniques takes place. Apart from his participation in online groups, Richard also attends training related to the upbringing of students with disabilities and has also led training in this area.

References

Abblett, M. (2021, November 22). *Mindful parenting: Meet your inner critic with self-compassion*. Mindful. https://www.mindful.org/mindful-parenting-meet-your-inner-critic-with-self-compassion/

Aletheia. (2021, August 3). *How to identify your emotional triggers (before it's too late)*. LonerWolf. https://lonerwolf.com/emotional-triggers/#h-11-signs-you-re-being-emotionally-triggered

Amen Clinics. (2020, January 2). *Which of the 5 types of dysfunctional families do you have?* Amen Clinics. https://www.amenclinics.com/blog/which-of-the-5-types-of-dysfunctional-families-do-you-have/

American Psychological Association. (2022, August 9). *Controlling anger—Before it controls you*. Https://Www.apa.org. https://www.apa.org/topics/anger/control

APA. (2022). *APA dictionary of psychology*. Dictionary.apa.org. https://dictionary.apa.org/dysfunctional-family

Barkley, S. (2022, June 27). *11 signs of an overwhelmed parent never to ignore*. Power of Positivity. https://www.powerofpositivity.com/overwhelmed-parent-signs/

Brandt, A. (2018, May 24). *4 ways to be kinder to yourself and build self-empathy.* Good Therapy. https://www.goodtherapy.org/blog/4-ways-to-be-kinder-to-yourself-build-self-empathy-0524185

Cleveland Clinic. (2020, May 20). *Intermittent explosive disorder.* Cleveland Clinic. https://my.clevelandclinic.org/health/diseases/17786-intermittent-explosive-disorder

Concordia University. (n.d.). *Examples of cognitive restructuring.* Www.concordia.ca. https://www.concordia.ca/cunews/offices/provost/health/topics/stress-management/cognitive-restructuring-examples.html#:~:text=Cognitive%20restructuring%20is%20a%20technique

Cook-Campbell, A. (2021, August 19). *Breathwork: The secret to emotional regulation.* Www.betterup.com. https://www.betterup.com/blog/breathwork#:~:text=Taking%20control%20of%20your%20breath

Cronkleton, E. (2019, April 9). *10 breathing exercises to try: For stress, training and lung capacity.* Healthline. https://www.healthline.com/health/breathing-exercise#alternate-nostril-breathing

Dadomo, H., Grecucci, A., Giardini, I., Ugolini, E., Carmelita, A., & Panzeri, M. (2016). Schema therapy for emotional dysregulation: Theoretical implication and clinical applications. *Frontiers in Psychology*, 7. https://doi.org/10.3389/fpsyg.2016.01987

Divecha, D. (2017, November 30). *Teenagers might have a problem with respect but it's not the one you think.* Developmental Science. https://www.developmentalscience.com/blog/2017/1 1/29/teenagers-might-have-a-problem-with-respect-but-its-not-the-one-you-think

Douglas, L. M. (2017, May 11). *10 signs you have a toxic parent.* HealthyWay. https://www.healthyway.com/content/signs-you-have-a-toxic-parent/

Finlay, L. (2012, November 15). *4 steps to letting go of the past.* Today's Parent. https://www.todaysparent.com/family/parenting/4-steps-to-letting-go-of-the-past/image/2/

5 tips for cultivating empathy. (2021, March). Harvard. https://mcc.gse.harvard.edu/resources-for-families/5-tips-cultivating-empathy

Gilles, G. (2015). *7 tips for effective communication with your school-aged child.* Mentalhelp.net. https://www.mentalhelp.net/blogs/7-tips-for-effective-communication-with-your-school-aged-child/

Godfrey, D. (2020, January 7). *Dealing with power struggles.* Positive Parenting. https://www.positiveparenting.com/dealing-with-power-struggles/

Good Reads. (n.d.-a). *A quote from The Wedding.* Www.goodreads.com.

https://www.goodreads.com/quotes/117907-what-it-s-like-to-be-a-parent-it-s-one-of

Good Reads. (n.d.-b). *Aristotle quote*. Www.goodreads.com. https://www.goodreads.com/author/show/2192.Aristotle

Good Reads. (n.d.-c). *Generational trauma quotes (9 quotes)*. Www.goodreads.com. https://www.goodreads.com/quotes/tag/generational-trauma

Good Reads. (n.d.-d). *Jill Bolte Taylor quote*. Www.goodreads.com. https://www.goodreads.com/author/show/82111.Jill_Bolte_Taylor

Good Reads. (n.d.-e). *Shannon L. Alder quote*. Www.goodreads.com. https://www.goodreads.com/author/show/1391130.Shannon_L_Alder

Good Reads. (n.d.-f). *T.F. Hodge quote*. Www.goodreads.com. https://www.goodreads.com/author/show/4636732.T_F_Hodge

Good Reads. (n.d.-g). *Toxic parents quotes by Susan Forward*. Www.goodreads.com. https://www.goodreads.com/work/quotes/3551-toxic-parents-overcoming-their-hurtful-legacy-and-reclaiming-your-life

Griffin, T. (2022, August 11). *Gain control of your emotions*. WikiHow. https://www.wikihow.com/Gain-Control-of-Your-Emotions

Hospital, B. R. B. (2021, May 6). *Identifying emotional triggers and what they mean*. Baton Rouge Behavioral Hospital. https://batonrougebehavioral.com/identifying-emotional-triggers-and-what-they-mean/

Jacobson, S. (2015, October 20). *Impulsivity—When you just can't stop yourself and it's ruining everything*. Harley Therapy™ Blog. https://www.harleytherapy.co.uk/counselling/what-is-impulsivity.htm

Kennedy, L. (2020, November 6). *11 positive parenting strategies you need to start using*. Www.prodigygame.com. https://www.prodigygame.com/main-en/blog/positive-parenting/

Kessler, D. (2018, March 13). *Why it is so important for parents to validate their children*. PsychAlive. https://www.psychalive.org/why-important-parents-validate-children/

LaScala, M. (2019, August 9). *The 40 best kids quotes, because raising children goes faster than you'd think*. Good Housekeeping. https://www.goodhousekeeping.com/life/parenting/g28541976/best-kids-quotes/

Lee, K. (2021, July 31). *Keep tone and words positive when communicating with your child*. Verywell Family. https://www.verywellfamily.com/how-do-you-talk-to-your-child-620058

Lewis, B. (2017, December 18). *Anger management: How food affects your mood*. Mind Body Seven.

https://www.mindbody7.com/news/2017/12/18/anger-management-how-food-affects-your-mood

Lewis, R. (2020, September 25). *Types of attachment: Avoidant, anxious, secure, and more.* Healthline. https://www.healthline.com/health/parenting/types-of-attachment#change

Li, P. (2022a, June 25). *9 critical reasons why punishment doesn't work for your child.* Parenting for Brain. https://www.parentingforbrain.com/why-punishment-doesnt-work/

Li, P. (2022b, July 9). *Emotional validation: How to validate a child's feelings (33 examples).* Parenting for Brain. https://www.parentingforbrain.com/emotional-validation/

Long, J. (n.d.). *Psychological safety: What our kids need most during the COVID-19 crisis.* Thriveglobal.com. https://thriveglobal.com/stories/psychological-safety-what-our-kids-need-most-during-the-covid-19-crisis/

Maria. (2018, July 12). *Feeling like an inadequate parent—How to cope.* Parent on Board. https://www.parentonboard.com/the-inadequate-parent/

Markham, L. (2014, January). *Punishment doesn't work.* Psychology Today. http://www.psychologytoday.com/blog/feeling-our-way/201401/punishment-doesnt-work

Martin, S. (2018, July 6). *The effects of growing up in a dysfunctional family.* Sharon Martin Counseling.

https://sharonmartincounseling.com/the-effects-of-growing-up-in-a-dysfunctional-family/

McCready, A. (2021, December 9). *Here's what makes "positive parenting" different—and why experts say it's one of the best parenting styles.* CNBC. https://www.cnbc.com/2021/12/04/why-psychologists-say-positive-parenting-is-the-best-style-for-raising-confident-successful-kids.html#:~:text=What%20is%20positive%20parenting?

Meleen, M. (n.d.). *10 unhealthy characteristics of a dysfunctional family.* LoveToKnow. https://family.lovetoknow.com/about-family-values/10-unhealthy-characteristics-dysfunctional-family

Mind Tools Content Team. (2014). *Cognitive restructuring: Reducing stress by changing your thinking.* Mindtools.com. https://www.mindtools.com/pages/article/newtcs_81.htm

Moore, C. (2019, June 2). *How to practice self-compassion: 8 Techniques and tips.* PositivePsychology.com. https://positivepsychology.com/how-to-practice-self-compassion/

Morin, A. (2021, June 20). *5 positive discipline strategies to change your child's behavior.* Verywell Family. https://www.verywellfamily.com/examples-of-positive-discipline-1095049#:~:text=The%20most%20effective%20positive%20discipline

Niebes-Davis, A. (2015, April 28). *Emotional check-ins: Why you need them.* Dr Allison Answers. https://drallisonanswers.com/mindfulness/the-power-of-emotional-check-ins-and-5-steps-to-help-you-get-started/

Nortje, A. (2020, June 5). *How to practice mindfulness: 10 practical steps and tips.* PositivePsychology.com. https://positivepsychology.com/how-to-practice-mindfulness/

Pace, A. (2019, March 6). *This is the crucial difference between positive and permissive parenting.* Parenting from the Heart. https://parentingfromtheheartblog.com/positive-parenting-permissive-parenting-2/

Parlakian, R. (2016, February 1). *How to help your child develop empathy.* Zero to Three. https://www.zerotothree.org/resource/how-to-help-your-child-develop-empathy/

Pearlstein, J. G., Johnson, S. L., Modavi, K., Peckham, A. D., & Carver, C. S. (2018). Neurocognitive mechanisms of emotion-related impulsivity: The role of arousal. *Society for Psychophysiological Research*, 56(2), e13293. https://doi.org/10.1111/psyp.13293

Pincus, D. (2019). *5 secrets for communicating with your teenager.* Empowering Parents. https://www.empoweringparents.com/article/5-secrets-for-communicating-with-teenagers/

Playful Notes. (2017, January 28). *12 inspiring positive parenting quotes that will warm your heart.* Playful Notes. https://playfulnotes.com/positive-parenting-quotes/

Raising Children Network. (2021, April 20). *Self-compassion for parents.* Raising Children Network. https://raisingchildren.net.au/grown-ups/looking-after-yourself/wellbeing/self-compassion-for-parents

Rapson, J. (2020, June 9). *10 quotes about parenting in anger every mom needs to read today.* For Every Mom. https://foreverymom.com/mom-gold/10-quotes-about-anger-in-parenting-every-mom-needs-to-read-today/

Richardson, J. M. (2021, July 19). *Why am I such an angry parent? And, what can I do about it?* A Fine Parent. https://afineparent.com/positive-parenting-faq/angry-parents.html

Ridgeview Behavioral Hospital. (2021, May 15). *How to identify emotional triggers in 3 steps.* Ridgeview Behavioral Hospital. https://ridgeviewhospital.net/how-to-identify-emotional-triggers-in-3-steps/

Salters-Pedneault, K. (2020, November 16). *Overwhelmed by emotion? This exercise helps you accept your feelings.* Verywell Mind. https://www.verywellmind.com/emotional-acceptance-exercise-observing-your-emotions-425373

Salters-Pedneault, K. (2022, March 24). *How to validate emotions with borderline personality disorder.* Verywell Mind. https://www.verywellmind.com/what-is-emotional-validation-

425336#:~:text=Emotional%20validation%20is%20the%20process

Santos-Longhurst, A. (2021, September 9). *Do I have anger issues? How to identify and treat an angry outlook.* Healthline. https://www.healthline.com/health/anger-issues#causes

Schenck, L. K. (2011, June 18). *Recognize your emotions in 6 steps.* Mindfulness Muse. https://www.mindfulnessmuse.com/dialectical-behavior-therapy/recognize-your-emotions-in-6-steps

Schwartz, A. N. (2010). *Revisiting your childhood home, "Remembrance of things past."* Mentalhelp.net. https://www.mentalhelp.net/blogs/revisiting-your-childhood-home-quot-remembrance-of-things-past-quot/

Shriver, M. (2018, October 7). *Why we all need to practice self-empathy.* Maria Shriver. https://mariashriver.com/why-we-all-need-to-practice-self-empathy/

Sonnier, M. (2012, January 6). *4 steps to address how you really feel.* Tiny Buddha. https://tinybuddha.com/blog/4-steps-to-address-how-you-really-feel/

Tackett, B. (2022, August 2). *Refusing to give in: 8 ways to beat cravings.* DrugAbuse.com. https://drugabuse.com/blog/beat-cravings/

thetherapistparent. (2020, August 13). *Why punishment doesn't work and what does.* The Therapist Parent. https://www.thetherapistparent.com/post/why-punishment-doesn-t-work-and-what-does

UNICEF. (n.d.). *How to communicate effectively with your young child*. Www.unicef.org. https://www.unicef.org/parenting/child-care/9-tips-for-better-communication

Villines, Z. (2022, June 19). *Cognitive restructuring: Steps, technique, and examples*. Www.medicalnewstoday.com. https://www.medicalnewstoday.com/articles/cognitive-restructuring#techniques

Vitality. (2020, May 27). *Owning your feelings*. Vitality. https://www.vitalitygroup.com/insights/owning-your-feelings/

Waheeda. (2021, September 3). *18 signs of bad parenting (and the bad effects) you'd wish you had known sooner*. Messy, yet Lovely. https://messyyetlovely.com/signs-of-bad-parenting/

Webb, J. (2022, January 23). *3 problems caused by ignoring your emotions*. Psychology Today. https://www.psychologytoday.com/us/blog/childhood-emotional-neglect/202201/3-problems-caused-ignoring-your-emotions

YouthAOD Toolbox. (n.d.). *The stages of an anger-related episode (the domino effect)*. Www.youthaodtoolbox.org.au. https://www.youthaodtoolbox.org.au/stages-anger-related-episode-domino-effect

Image References

Cameron, J. M. (2020). *Boy in yellow crew neck t-shirt sitting on chair* [Online Image]. In Pexels. https://www.pexels.com/photo/boy-in-yellow-crew-neck-t-shirt-sitting-on-chair-4144099/

Chai, S. (2021a). *Mother embracing baby tenderly in bedroom* [Online Image]. In Pexels. https://www.pexels.com/photo/mother-embracing-baby-tenderly-in-bedroom-7282279/

Chai, S. (2021b). *Young working mother cuddling baby and using laptop at home* [Online Image]. In Pexels. https://www.pexels.com/photo/young-working-mother-cuddling-baby-and-using-laptop-at-home-7282818/

Chernaya, K. (2020). *Tired mother with cute daughter resting on bed in cozy room* [Online Image]. In Pexels. https://www.pexels.com/photo/tired-mother-with-cute-daughter-resting-on-bed-in-cozy-room-4740574/

de Richelieu, A. (2020). *Father talking to his son* [Online Image]. In Pexels. https://www.pexels.com/photo/father-talking-to-his-son-4260102/

Grabowska, K. (2020). *Cute girl in gray dress laughing* [Online Image]. In Pexels. https://www.pexels.com/photo/cute-girl-in-gray-dress-laughing-6255691/

Grabowska, K. (2021a). *A mother getting upset to her daughter* [Online Image]. In Pexels. https://www.pexels.com/photo/a-mother-getting-upset-to-her-daughter-6957249/

Grabowska, K. (2021b). *Close-up shot of woman looking lonely* [Online Image]. In Pexels. https://www.pexels.com/photo/close-up-shot-of-woman-looking-lonely-7273324/

Lach, R. (2021). *Mother and daughter drawing together* [Online Image]. In Pexels. https://www.pexels.com/photo/mother and daughter-drawing-together-9872953/

Monstera. (2021). *Faceless people scolding discontent black girl* [Online Image]. In Pexels. https://www.pexels.com/photo/faceless-people-scolding-discontent-black-girl-7114755/

Nilov, M. (2021). *A man meditating* [Online Image]. In Pexels. https://www.pexels.com/photo/a-man-meditating-7530008/

Nothing Ahead. (2021). *Computer laptop on wooden table* [Online Image]. In Pexels. https://www.pexels.com/photo/computer-laptop-on-wooden-table-8365541/

Piacquadio, A. (2020). *Cheerful mother and daughter having fun on bed at home* [Online Image]. In Pexels. https://www.pexels.com/photo/cheerful-mother-and-daughter-having-fun-on-bed-at-home-3756036/

Sang-ngern, P. (2020a). *Crop woman with heart on palms* [Online Image]. In Pexels. https://www.pexels.com/photo/crop-woman-with-heart-on-palms-5340280/

Sang-ngern, P. (2020b). *Smiling crop woman with crossed hands* [Online Image]. In Pexels. https://www.pexels.com/photo/smiling-crop-woman-with-crossed-hands-5340278/

SHVETS Production. (2021). *Man soothing crying sad woman* [Online Image]. In Pexels. https://www.pexcls.com/photo/man-soothing-crying-sad-woman-on-sofa-7176216/

Снежана. (2019). *Woman walking behind toddler* [Online Image]. In Pexels. https://www.pexels.com/photo/woman-walking-behind-toddler-2310609/

Subiyanto, K. (2020). *Photo of woman and girl talking while lying on bed* [Online Image]. In Pexels. https://www.pexels.com/photo/photo-of-woman-and-girl-talking-while-lying-on-bed-4473774/

Summer, L. (2021a). *Emotional black woman yelling* [Online Image]. In Pexels. https://www.pexels.com/photo/emotional-black-woman-yelling-and-touching-head-6382714/

Summer, L. (2021b). *Multiracial ladies having disagreement in light room at home* [Online Image]. In Pexels. https://www.pexels.com/photo/multiracial-ladies-having-disagreement-in-light-room-at-home-6383204/

Summer, L. (2021c). *Unrecognizable woman having dispute with crop person* [Online Image]. In Pexels. https://www.pexels.com/photo/unrecognizable-woman-having-dispute-with-crop-person-6382709/

Made in United States
Troutdale, OR
03/02/2024

18085504R00101